SIMI

SAVORING SIMI: SINCE 1876

SIMI

SAVORING SIMI: SINCE 1876

Recipes and Stories from the Heart of Sonoma County

BY KOLIN VAZZOLER

from the SIMI Winery Kitchen

Recipe Photographs by Dan Mills

CONTENTS

SIMI HISTORY AT A GLANCE

1850s
Giuseppe Simi leaves his home in Tuscany to find fortune in the goldfields of California. Disillusioned with mining, he turns to farming, and then he and his brother, Pietro, become successful grocers in San Francisco.

1876
The Simi brothers produce their first wine in San Francisco from grapes purchased from the area around Healdsburg in Sonoma County.

1881
To accommodate their growing wine business, the brothers buy a winery in Healdsburg and a large tract of land north of town. They begin construction on a second winery and plant vineyards on the newly purchased land.

1890
Immigrant construction workers complete the first half of SIMI's stone cellars, which SIMI still uses today for winemaking.

1904
The expansion of the SIMI wine cellars is completed by Italian stonemasons. SIMI sits on a railway that connects Northern California to San Francisco. The strategic location is a boon for shipping wine to the bustling city.

1904
The Simi brothers die from influenza. Giuseppe's eighteen-year-old daughter, Isabelle, takes over management of the winery for the next sixty-six years. Isabelle marries a local Healdsburg banker, Fred R. Haigh, in 1908.

1920
The Volstead Act is passed and Prohibition begins. Anticipating a quick repeal, Isabelle and Fred continue to make wines every year, some of which are sold for medicinal and sacramental purposes. They sell vineyard holdings to generate income.

1933
Prohibition is repealed and SIMI has five hundred thousand gallons of cellared wine. Older vintages were used to produce brandy and vinegar while the newer vintages were sold to the thirsty public. Isabelle plants redwood trees at the winery in celebration.

1934
Isabelle establishes the first tasting room at SIMI, a roadside visitor's center fashioned from a twenty-five-thousand-gallon wine cask.

1941
SIMI wins gold medals for its Cabernet, Zinfandel, and Burgundy and a silver medal for its Pink Champagne in the prestigious California State Fair.

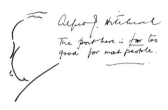

1950s and 60s

Isabelle and Fred's daughter, Vivien, joins the winery. Fred dies in 1954, and the mother and daughter continue to run SIMI in the burgeoning Sonoma wine country. They entertain many visitors, including such Hollywood notables as actor Joseph Cotten and film director Alfred Hitchcock. Vivien dies in 1968.

1970

A new tasting room is built, replacing Isabelle's giant-cask tasting room. Isabelle Simi retires, selling the winery to Alexander Valley grape grower Russell Green. She continues to greet winery visitors and work in the tasting room until her death in 1981.

1973

SIMI hires MaryAnn Graf, the country's first female enology graduate, as winemaker. She works closely with famed winemaker André Tchelistcheff, who consults for the winery.

1979

Winemaker Zelma Long joins SIMI and directs a major renovation of the winery's fermentation and barrel rooms, bringing the winery to national prominence again.

1983

SIMI engages Mary Evely, becoming one of the first California wineries to hire a full-time chef.

1984

SIMI begins developing Landslide Vineyard in Alexander Valley, which becomes a centerpiece of the winery's Cabernet Sauvignon program.

1989

With the acquisition of one hundred acres in the Russian River Valley, SIMI launches the development of Goldfields Vineyard, planted primarily to heritage clones of Chardonnay.

1990

SIMI celebrates one hundred years of making wine and builds a new hospitality center, located amid the redwood trees planted by Isabelle Simi.

2000

Susan Lueker joins SIMI and becomes director of winemaking, leading both the vineyard and the winemaking team.

2016

SIMI celebrates 140 years of winemaking as the oldest continuously operating winery in Sonoma County.

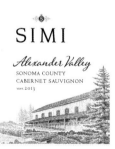

SIMI WINERY HISTORY AND HERITAGE

The remarkable history of SIMI Winery begins in the gold rush and spans the California wine boom of the nineteenth century, the thirteen-year-long Prohibition of the early twentieth century, and the reemergence of California winemaking as a thriving modern industry. Founded in 1876 by Giuseppe and Pietro Simi, SIMI has the distinction of being the oldest continuously operating winery in Sonoma County. It has never missed a harvest, not even during Prohibition, and it continues to produce wine out of its century-old stone cellar in Healdsburg.

FROM GOLD TO GRAPES

SIMI's story begins with Giuseppe Simi, who emigrated from Italy to the United States in the mid-nineteenth century and landed in California, drawn like so many others to the siren call of the state's gold rush. But Giuseppe's fortune was not to be made in gold, so he and his brother, Pietro, turned to farming and to establishing a fruit and vegetable business in San Francisco. In 1876, lured by the promise of California's burgeoning wine industry, the brothers made their first wine from grapes grown near the town of Healdsburg and transported by train to their home in San Francisco's North Beach.

The wine business took off, and in 1881, the brothers moved their wine production to an existing winery in Healdsburg and paid $2,250 in "gold coin" for 126 acres north of town, where they planted Zinfandel vines and began construction of a new winery. Giuseppe, who moved to Healdsburg with his family, was clever. In exchange for an easement that allowed the Northwestern Pacific Railroad to run through his property, the railroad company cleared and mined the basalt stone that he and Pietro used to build their winery. It was a win-win for the brothers, as the on-site depot made it easy to transport their wine to San Francisco for bottling and distribution.

TUSCAN ROOTS

When their dreams of finding gold in California were frustrated, Pietro and Giuseppe Simi turned to farming, a pursuit more familiar to the brothers, who were natives of Italy's Tuscany region. They sourced their first grapes, Zinfandel and Cabernet Sauvignon, from vineyards close to Healdsburg in what is now known as the Alexander Valley. With its rolling landscape of hills and valleys, the area is said to have reminded Giuseppe of his homeland, and when he and Pietro founded their winery, they called it Montepulciano, after the hillside town in Tuscany. The name SIMI wasn't used on the wines until after Prohibition.

A WINERY ON THE RAILROAD

The Simi brothers chose the winery site just north of Healdsburg for its strategic location on the Northwestern Pacific Railroad, which connected San Francisco Bay to the wine country and ran right through their property.

A QUEEN BEGINS HER REIGN

In 1904, Giuseppe and Pietro's wine operation was enjoying steady success when tragedy struck. The brothers died within four weeks of each other from influenza. It was Isabelle Simi, Giuseppe's eighteen-year-old daughter, who took over the management of the winery. Isabelle had worked closely with her father for several years (she once commented that she was weighing grapes at age twelve) and knew how to operate a winery. She had also recently been crowned Queen of Healdsburg at the annual Floral Festival, a great honor involving a parade that drew thousands. Her photos even appeared in the society sections of San Francisco newspapers. It was evident that Isabelle loved Healdsburg and the town loved her. Despite her youth, she was determined to keep SIMI in business.

By 1905, SIMI wines were sold primarily through the California Wine Association, a conglomerate that purchased wines in bulk and distributed them throughout the state, though the winery also dealt directly with distributors and restaurants in midwestern and eastern cities. In addition to her winemaking duties, Isabelle became involved in sales and distribution, and in 1908 she and a female cousin traveled to Colorado, Arizona, and New York to call on SIMI's distributors. In a taped interview late in her life, Isabelle recalled this trip—unusual for two young, unescorted women at the time—recounting how she and her cousin were "wined and dined" at some of the finest restaurants in the cities they visited.

In 1908, Isabelle married Fred R. Haigh, a Healdsburg local who worked as a cashier at the regional bank. Over the next decade Isabelle and Fred acquired land, planted vineyards,

This allowed SIMI to transport its wines easily to the booming Northern California city. The railroad tracks can still be seen today bordering the front of the winery's original stone cellar, though this section of the railway hasn't been used since the 1950s.

GIANT CASK TASTING ROOM

When Prohibition was repealed in 1933, SIMI had several hundred thousand cases of wine to sell but few outlets through which to sell them. Isabelle Simi Haigh, who ran the winery from 1904 to 1970, had a novel idea. To make sure that pass-ersby would know that SIMI had wine available for purchase, she created one of Sonoma County's first tasting rooms, setting a giant 25,000-gallon wine cask on its side for the purpose. The cask, which sat at the winery's entrance at the edge of Healdsburg Avenue, served as the SIMI tasting room for over thirty years. Photographs from the 1940s show a Bell telephone sign affixed to the cask, indicating it was also one of the few places in the area to make a telephone call in those days!

and even purchased another winery to handle their increasing production. At one time, SIMI was making or storing wine in three locations in Healdsburg. Years later, Isabelle estimated that SIMI had an annual production of about five hundred thousand gallons prior to Prohibition.

SURVIVING PROHIBITION

In 1920, the Volstead Act passed, prohibiting "the sale, production, importation, and transportation of alcoholic beverages." Not surprisingly, the next thirteen years proved difficult. Convinced that Prohibition would not last, Isabelle and Fred continued to produce wine every year, hiding it away within the vast stone cellar. Bills of sale indicate that SIMI sold small amounts for medicinal and sacramental purposes, but most of it simply sat in the winery awaiting the end of the legislation.

Isabelle and Fred were forced to sell some of their vineyard land in order to make ends meet, and some of the wine they made became too old to sell. Nevertheless, when Prohibition was finally repealed in late 1933, they were ready with several hundred thousand gallons of perfectly aged wine. Ever the entrepreneur and always looking for new ways to increase distribution, Isabelle had an empty 25,000-gallon redwood wine cask hauled up from the cellar to the front of the winery and set on its side, where it served as a tasting room. It was one of the first tasting rooms in Sonoma County, and through Isabelle's vivacious personality (in the early days, she reportedly flagged down passing cars, urging passengers to stop and taste), it was one of the county's most successful.

A KNACK FOR PROMOTION

Over the next couple of decades, SIMI wines continued to gain renown. In the late 1930s and early 1940s, Hotel Del Monte, a luxury hotel in Monterey, California, located on what is now Pebble Beach, served SIMI as its "house" red. It was excellent exposure, as hotel guests would often stop by the winery to purchase the wine whenever they were in Sonoma County. In 1941, Isabelle and Fred, at the insistence of their distributor,

THE OLD STONE WINERY

SIMI's old stone winery is actually two buildings that share a common wall. The three-story southern half was completed in 1890, built by immigrants who had worked on the First Transcontinental Railroad. The northern half, completed in 1904, was built by Italian stonemasons. In an era without pumps or ready access to electricity, both sides of the winery were constructed so wine could be moved via gravity: grapes were crushed on the top floor, lowered to the second floor for fermentation, and finally to the bottom floor for aging. Today, SIMI continues to use this historic cellar for wine storage and production, the thick stone walls providing a naturally cool environment for the wines that rest within.

SIMI VINEYARD

ORIGINAL HOTEL DEL MONTE 1880

HOTEL DEL MONTE
SELECTION

SONOMA
CABERNET

ALCOHOL 12% BY VOLUME

entered SIMI wines into the California State Fair wine competition. Against forty competitors, SIMI won four top awards, including gold medals for its Cabernet, Zinfandel, and Burgundy and a silver medal for its Pink Champagne. Soon many fine restaurants in Sonoma and San Francisco were carrying SIMI wines.

But SIMI's stellar reputation was based on more than good promotion. From the beginning, Giuseppe had insisted that the grapes used in SIMI's wines measure at least 22 degrees Brix, a level of sugar that assured plenty of flavor and adequate alcohol. He also insisted that the wines age for at least five to seven years prior to release, and that varietal-labeled wine, such as Cabernet Sauvignon, be 100 percent composed of those grapes. All of these parameters, which were steadfastly upheld by Isabelle through her years of ownership, contributed to SIMI's solid reputation and attracted attention and praise not only from such celebrities as actor Joseph Cotten and film director Alfred Hitchcock but also from fellow winemakers such as Louis Martini.

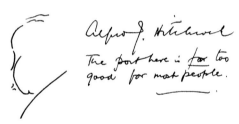

Alfred J. Hitchcock
The port here is far too
good for most people.

A DAUGHTER STEPS IN

It was during the post-Prohibition period that Isabelle and Fred asked their daughter, Vivien, a high school teacher, to help run the winery. World War II had brought changes in distribution, and the Hotel Del Monte, which had been so important to the winery's growing fame, closed down in 1942. Money was tight, Fred was in ill health, and Isabelle was preoccupied with running the tasting room. Vivien agreed, and when Fred died in 1954, she assumed even greater responsibility, working side by side with her mother on business matters and initiating the hiring of a winemaker, Alex Podgorny. At the time, SIMI's best-selling wines were Cabernet, Carignane, Pinot Noir, Petite Sirah, and Zinfandel. There was a brief attempt to revive the winery's once thriving sparkling wine business, though it proved unsuccessful. With fewer and fewer outlets for the wine and little money for investment, production began to drop.

THE REDWOOD GROVE

Visitors to SIMI Winery are always struck by the majestic redwood trees that stand near the winery's fountain area. They look like they've been there for centuries, but they were actually planted by Isabelle Simi in celebration of Prohibition's repeal. She is said to have commented "As long as they're here, we're going to be here." The trees will no doubt continue to provide a shaded, peaceful resting spot for visitors to the winery for many generations to come.

Facing page (clockwise from top): The giant cask tasting room;. visitors sample SIMI wines; a 1941 SIMI Cabernet wine label sporting a picture of the Hotel Del Monte; the Simi family—daughter Vivian (center) with parents Fred and Isabelle.

Above (clockwise from top): Isabelle Simi's parents, Giuseppe and Nicoletta; Isabelle Simi, age eighteen, recently crowned as the Queen of Healdsburg; crowds gather as the queen's horse-drawn float passes during Healdsburg's Floral Festival parade, circa 1904.

Since 1876

Above (clockwise from top): A wine label shows Simi's old stone winery and giant cask tasting room; Isabelle Simi and Fred Haigh pose with visitors in front of their winery's giant cask tasting room; Isabelle with new owner Russell Green, 1970; Isabelle wearing her signature button collection on her work apron in the 1970s; the Simi-Haigh family–daughter Vivian (left) with parents Fred and Isabelle in the late 1940s.

Above (from top): Winemaker MaryAnn Graf with André Tchelistcheff; SIMI 1974 Alexander Valley Cabernet Sauvignon; winemaker Zelma Long; former SIMI winery owners BJ and Russell Green, at SIMI's 135th anniversary celebration.

In 1968, Vivien passed away, leaving Isabelle no heirs to run the winery. In 1970, she sold SIMI to Russell and BJ Green, neighbors and Alexander Valley grape growers who often visited Isabelle and the winery. Before transferring ownership, Isabelle was instrumental in the design of the tasting room, the rustic yet elegant building that continues to welcome SIMI visitors today. In the decade following the sale, Isabelle continued to work in the tasting room six or seven days a week as a greeter, telling stories and sharing the wines she knew and loved so well. Isabelle retired from the winery in 1980, and passed away in 1981 at the age of ninety-five.

A NEW ERA

Russell and BJ Green's ownership ushered in a new era at SIMI, one that aligned with the renaissance that was happening in Northern California's wine industry. With a new source of capital, the winery was able to update its facilities and vineyards, build the new tasting room, and explore new winemaking and growing techniques that resulted in higher-quality wines. In 1973, SIMI hired MaryAnn Graf as winemaker. MaryAnn was the first female graduate of the Viticulture and Enology program at the University of California, Davis, and was the only female winemaker in the United States when she began her tenure at SIMI. She had the privilege of working closely with influential winemaker André Tchelistcheff, who consulted for SIMI and became one of her great mentors. Mary Ann also created the first SIMI wine, a 1974 Cabernet Sauvignon, to carry the Alexander Valley appellation on its label.

In 1979, Zelma Long was named SIMI's winemaker, lured away from Robert Mondavi Winery where she had served as chief enologist. Zelma was the second female graduate of the UC Davis Viticulture and Enology program and spent the next twenty years at SIMI. A steady presence under subsequent ownership changes, she oversaw both winemaking and grape growing and earned successive promotions to president and CEO. Under her leadership, SIMI's facilities were further upgraded with

A HISTORY OF WOMEN WINEMAKERS

Since 1904, SIMI has never been without a female winemaker on its staff. It began with Isabelle Simi, who ran the winery for sixty-six years from 1904 to 1970. The female legacy continues to this day with Director of Winemaking Susan Lueker (above), who joined the winery in 2000 and oversees a winemaking and cellar staff comprised largely of women, including Winemaker Lisa Evich (left). Notably, the winery also hired both the first and the second female graduates of the esteemed Viticulture and Enology program at UC Davis: MaryAnn Graf in 1973 and Zelma Long in 1979.

the retrofit of the winery's old stone cellar and the construction of a new fermentation cellar. Zelma also significantly expanded and upgraded SIMI's vineyard holdings, beginning in 1982 with the development of the southern Alexander Valley site that would become SIMI's Landslide Vineyard, and later, in 1989, with the development of the Goldfields Vineyard in the Russian River Valley. Today SIMI utilizes fruit from both of these vineyards for its most revered wines, including the Landslide Vineyard Alexander Valley Cabernet Sauvignon and the Russian River Valley Chardonnay Reserve.

LANDSLIDE VINEYARD

SIMI's gorgeous Landslide Vineyard in Alexander Valley comprises three different elevations with five distinct soil types, yielding grapes with a spectrum of flavors that contribute to complex vineyard-designated wines. Developed in the 1980s, Landslide is planted entirely to red grapes, all five Bordeaux varieties and a little Tannat. The vineyard's name is derived from an ancient volcanic landslide that changed the flow of the Russian River.

A TRADITION OF WINE
AND FOOD

Given the Simi family's Tuscan roots, it's no wonder that the winery has a reputation for creating wines meant to be enjoyed with food. It was a natural for Isabelle Simi, who often served guests and visitors to the winery meals that complemented her wines. In the early 1980s, SIMI was one of the first wineries in the wine country to offer food pairing suggestions on the front labels of its wine bottles.

PIONEERS IN WINE AND FOOD

With the advancement of California's wine culture in the 1970s and 1980s came a parallel interest in fine food, and the concept of wine and food pairing was soon a subject of increased exploration. SIMI had long recognized that wine was best enjoyed with food, and Isabelle reportedly cooked and served meals to guests from a bar built in the middle of her living room. In 1983, the winery hired Mary Evely, who became one of the first full-time winery chefs in California. Chef Evely, who spent the next eighteen years at SIMI, is still widely recognized as a pioneer in the field of pairing wine and food. In her time at the winery, she developed The Vintner's Table, a groundbreaking educational wine and food program that became the basis for her book, *The Vintner's Table Cookbook*, published by SIMI in 1998. The book, which included an extensive wine and food pairing guide as well as dozens of recipes organized by the varietals with which they are served, won the prestigious First Book: Julia Child Award.

In 1990, SIMI celebrated one hundred years of winemaking in its original stone cellars, and the winery completed construction of a new hospitality center, replacing Isabelle's original cask tasting room. Built to house SIMI's growing hospitality and education programs, the center's tasting room pays homage to the original with a ceiling of wooden staves that imitates the inside of a wine barrel. The dining room boasts a cathedral-like ceiling, a nod to the winery's history of making sacramental wines during Prohibition. SIMI continues to use the hospitality center for tastings, educational programs, demonstrations, and special meals and events.

Right: Guests enjoy wine and food al fresco in SIMI's redwood grove around the fountain and in the hospitality center's cathedral-ceilinged dining room.

FARM-TO-TABLE DINING

Upon Chef Evely's retirement in 2001, SIMI hired Eric Lee, a graduate of the Culinary Institute of America. Chef Lee and SIMI's vineyard team set aside a half acre of the Landslide Vineyard for a garden, to create farm-to-table meals for the winery's guests and employees. That garden, along with planters strategically placed on the winery's grounds in Healdsburg, continues to fuel SIMI's wine and food programs, now run by Kolin Vazzoler (above), who was named executive chef in 2012. Chef Vazzoler not only relies on the garden's bounty for his recipes but also actively sources meats and supplemental produce from local farmers. He believes in making his own kitchen staples whenever possible as well, churning fresh butter from local dairy cream, milling flour for his pastas and breads, and preserving fruits and vegetables for future use.

TRADITION AND INNOVATION

Today, with over six hundred acres of estate vineyards in Sonoma County, including property in the most prominent regions of the Alexander Valley and the Russian River Valley, SIMI's winemaking is overseen by Director of Winemaking Susan Lueker, who upholds the winery's long tradition of creating red, white, and rosé wines of exceptional flavor, balance, and finesse. Like her predecessors, Susan brings a thorough knowledge of both winemaking and grape growing to her role and ensures that the wines SIMI produces carry the stamp of the land. The wines being created today are better than ever, a reflection of the special vineyards in which they are grown and the tremendous attention to detail with which they are crafted. As the winery looks forward to its next century of winemaking, the pioneering spirit of exploration and adventure continues to drive the people of SIMI, just as it drove the founders so many years ago. The story of SIMI is still being written.

GOLDFIELDS VINEYARD

Developed in the late 1980s by SIMI's former winemaker, Zelma Long, Goldfields Vineyard in the Russian River Valley is planted to a variety of Chardonnay rootstocks, field selections, and clones sourced from some of the best and oldest vineyards in California, including Calera and Mount Eden. The vineyard's prized Goldridge and Huichica soils provide superb drainage, while its ideal location in a slightly warmer region of this cool appellation allows the grapes to ripen fully each vintage.

WINE AND FOOD:
UNCOVERING THE MYSTERY TO PERFECT PAIRINGS

When Mary Evely, SIMI's chef from 1983 to 2001, published *The Vintner's Table Cookbook: Recipes from a Winery Chef*, the subject of wine and food pairing was still relatively new. Written in the late 1990s, Evely's book was groundbreaking in its own way, offering readers insights into all she had learned about matching wine and food. Since then, wine and food pairing has been the topic of dozens of books, articles, and treatises. Readers continue to seek knowledge on how to choose what wine to drink with what food and vice versa.

But what if it was simpler? What if you could choose the wines and the foods you like and simply enjoy them together? At SIMI, we think you can. You see, the word pairing implies that a certain wine must be served with a particular type of food. Sometimes that works, but we've found that many traditional wine and food pairing "rules" are too constrictive and are often misguided or even wrong. In reality, enjoying wine and food together is not that complicated and can nearly always be achieved by adjusting and balancing the taste (not the flavor) of the food you want to serve.

WINE AS THE WINEMAKER INTENDED

If you ask a winery chef about his or her philosophy when it comes to wine and food, you will invariably hear that the wine comes first. The winery chef's task, after all, is to prepare foods that allow the wine to shine. The food should never overshadow or change the wine in any way; rather, the wine should always taste just as the winemaker intended. At SIMI, we make wines specifically to be enjoyed with food, with an exquisite balance of fruit, acid, tannin, and alcohol. Leaving the wine as our winemaker intended means that it should have the same taste profile, the same balance, both before and after the food is tasted. In our discussion of wine and food, this is the one rule to which we adhere: the wine must be relatively unchanged by the food.

SIMI WINES AND BALANCE

Perhaps it's our Italian heritage, but at SIMI we've always adhered to the philosophy that wine is meant to be enjoyed with food. To that end, we strive to create wines that naturally work with food, wines that have an impeccable balance of fruit and acid, alcohol, and tannin. We achieve this through our vineyard practices and our winemaking techniques, picking our grapes at the precise moment of ripeness, using a mixture of new and seasoned oak barrels for aging and fermentation, and blending lots to create complementary flavors and a balance of tastes. Paying close attention to all of these details results in food-friendly wines that enhance the dining experience, whether you're here at the winery, out at a restaurant, or enjoying a meal at home.

WINE AND CHEESE

Many cheeses are high in umami, which can throw some wines out of balance. For instance, Parmesan cheese can accentuate the bitterness of the tannins in a Cabernet Sauvignon to the wine's detriment. But don't despair. When using cheese in a recipe, be mindful of its umami and add a counterbalancing ingredient with salt (such as capers or anchovies) and/or acid (lemon juice or vinegar) to the dish. If you are serving a cheese course, offer a wine that is lower in tannin and higher in acid, such as Sauvignon Blanc, Pinot Noir, or a sparkling wine.

What this means in practical terms is that cooks preparing foods to serve with wine must look at the basic tastes of the food—umami, sweet, salty, sour, and bitter—and adjust them according to the wine being served. The umami taste, present in all delicious ingredients, and the sweet taste must be balanced by both the salty and the acidic taste. If the appropriate balance is not in place within the food, the wine will be thrown out of balance. But if the proportion of these tastes within the food is adjusted correctly, any wine, regardless of its type, can be enjoyed with the food.

THE EFFECT OF UMAMI AND SWEETNESS

Umami, which some people refer to as the "delicious" taste in food, is known to trigger taste receptors in the mouth and make food taste better. Foods high in umami include shellfish, cured meats, asparagus, mushrooms, tomatoes, cheeses, and soy sauce. But here's the hitch: both the umami taste and the sweet taste have a dramatic effect on the taste and balance of wine.

If a dish is high in umami or sweetness, it will make the wine taste stronger. That is, it will amplify your perception of the wine's acidity to a higher level of tartness, make the tannins in red wine seem more astringent or bitter, and increase the sensation of alcohol on the palate. Foods high in umami or sweetness will also suppress a wine's lovely fruit flavors. We've probably all had the experience of toasting a new bride and groom with sparkling wine and a piece of wedding cake. Unless the sparkling wine is off-dry, its fruit is completely obliterated by the sweetness of the cake. In other words, umami and sweetness can throw a wine completely out of balance, making it almost unrecognizable.

ADJUST THE TASTE OF THE FOOD TO GO WITH THE WINE

If this sounds complicated, here's what you need to know. You can counteract these stronger tastes caused by umami and sweetness by adjusting the salt and acid in your food. By adding a pinch of salt or a salty ingredient and a squeeze of lemon or a dash of vinegar (choose the vinegar carefully, as some, like balsamic, are sweet and loaded with umami)

to the food, any increase in the tartness, astringency, or burn of the wine caused by the umami or sweetness of the food will be neutralized, and the wine's balance and fruit flavors will return.

Conversely, if you have a food that is high in acid and/or salt, the wine you serve it with will taste milder. The perception of its acidity and tannin will be significantly reduced and the wine may taste flat or flabby. In this case, adding ingredients to the dish that increase its umami and/or sweetness—a sprinkling of Parmesan cheese, for example, or a slightly sweet fruit—will return the wine to balance.

Making these small adjustments to the foods you plan to serve with wine is easy. It can take place in the kitchen as the food is prepared, or tableside with a squeeze of lemon and a pinch of salt. You may need to experiment to see what works. If a food unexpectedly makes a wine you like taste unpleasant, season the food as suggested here and you'll likely enjoy the wine once again.

PLAY WITH FLAVORS

Now for the fun part! Once the taste of the food has been adjusted and balanced for maximum enjoyment with the wine, there are many ways to add interest and spark to the tasting experience. This is where flavor comes in, and where some of the "old" rules about wine and food, such as finding flavor affinities between certain wines and foods, can be useful as guidelines. What follows is a list of common varietals with food flavor suggestions that many people find to be pleasing. Note that it's not the color or the main type of food (meat, fish, poultry) that's important here; instead, it's how the dish is seasoned and accompanied. And remember, these are only suggestions, as flavor preference and sensitivity are entirely subjective. Not everyone will show the same partiality for enjoying certain types of wines with specific flavors in food. However, once the umami, sweetness, saltiness, and acid of the food are balanced with the wine, creating harmony among the flavors of the wine and food can make an experience go from very good to simply sublime.

UMAMI, THE FIFTH TASTE

Umami is one of the five basic tastes, an addition to the more commonly recognized tastes of sweet, salty, sour, and bitter. It was first detected in 1907 by a Japanese chemist, Professor Kikunae Ikeda of the Tokyo Imperial University, when he tasted the crystalline remains of evaporated seaweed broth. Umami is present in foods high in glutamate, a type of amino acid, and is often described as a pleasant meaty or mouthwatering taste that coats the palate and rounds out or balances the flavors in food. It occurs naturally in foods such as tomatoes, mushrooms, soy sauce, shellfish, and cheese, but can also be enhanced through such cooking methods as roasting, grilling, and caramelizing.

SIP, TASTE, SIP

To understand how the taste of umami interacts with wine, you can try this simple experiment. Grill an unseasoned piece of beef (or an unseasoned portobello mushroom lightly basted with olive oil) until medium-rare or medium, transfer it to a plate, and set a slice of lemon and some salt nearby. Pour a white or red wine (or both). Taste the wine, being careful to notice the balance of fruit, acid, tannin, and alcohol. Now take a bite of the meat (or mushroom). Taste the wine again. You will probably notice that the wine doesn't taste quite the same. It may seem less fruity to you and more acidic or sour. The alcohol may stand out more, and the tannin may be accentuated.

Taste the wine again. Season the meat (or mushroom) with a little salt and a spritz of the lemon, take a bite, and then taste the wine again. This time you should notice that the wine tastes much as it did before you tasted the meat. The balance of fruit, acid, tannin, and alcohol should be restored. By adding a little bit of salt and acid to your food, you've counterbalanced the umami and restored the wine to its original balance.

THE ROLE OF TEXTURE

Paying attention to the different textures of wine and food is also instructive. Texture can refer to the sensory element of touch—thin or fatty, crisp or velvety, smooth or crunchy—or of temperature—cold, warm, or hot. Either aligning or contrasting the textures of wine and food can be a pleasing way to add interest to a pairing. Again, as long as the taste of the food is appropriately balanced, it will be enjoyable with almost any wine. Here are four examples:

Light foods with light wines
(poached fish with Sauvignon Blanc or unoaked Chardonnay)

Rich foods with rich wines
(a well-marbled steak with a concentrated Cabernet Sauvignon)

Rich, fatty, or fried foods with higher acid wines
(fried calamari with mouthwatering Sauvignon Blanc or sparkling wine)

Moderately hot, spicy foods with off-dry wines
(Thai or Indian food with Riesling, Moscato, or Gewürztraminer)

COMMON VARIETALS WITH COMPLEMENTARY FOOD FLAVORS

Sauvignon Blanc	Bay leaf, bell pepper, citrus, coriander, dill, eggplant, garlic, olive oil, onions, oregano, parsley, rosemary, tarragon, tomato
Chardonnay	Butter, citrus, fennel seed, ginger, sweet vegetables (corn, carrots, peas), sorrel, tarragon
Pinot Grigio	Citrus, fresh herbs (basil, cilantro, chervil, dill, parsley, tarragon, thyme), lemongrass, garlic
Riesling, Gewürztraminer	Corn, nuts, smoked foods, spicy cuisine such as Asian and Tex-Mex, tree fruits
Pinot Noir, Sangiovese	Allspice, aniseed, balsamic vinegar, basil, cinnamon, cherry, clove, fennel seed, garlic, mushroom, nutmeg, olive, oregano, plum, rosemary, sage, soy sauce, spearmint, tomato
Zinfandel, Syrah	Aniseed, basil, berry, black cherry, clove, fennel seed, mushroom, olive, onion, oregano, peppercorns (green, black), sage, smoked meats, tomato salsa
Cabernet Sauvignon, Merlot, Malbec	Bay leaf, basil, dark chocolate, green pepper, mint, olive, oregano, rosemary, tarragon

PERSONAL PREFERENCE IS RULE NO. 1

Any discussion of wine and food is incomplete without noting the role of personal preference. No matter how good a black olive pesto–topped pizzetta tastes with a SIMI Pinot Noir, if your guest doesn't like olives, the combination isn't going to work. Always keep in mind that the purpose of wine and food is not to sit down to the "perfect" meal but to make every meal an enjoyable experience. The goal is to relax, discover, and appreciate the camaraderie.

ABOUT THE RECIPES

The recipes in this book are a collection of our favorites at SIMI Winery created by chefs throughout our history. These are the recipes we continue to enjoy, the ones that allow SIMI wines to be as fresh, balanced, flavorful, and complex as our winemakers intend them to be. In creating and revising these recipes, we've adhered to the principles of wine and food enjoyment outlined in this chapter, and making the recipes as directed will result in dishes that are perfectly balanced for the wines we've suggested as enjoyable partners. However, you may decide to switch it up. Perhaps you'd like to serve the Arugula, Corn, and Red Pepper Salad with a Pinot Noir rather than the suggested Sauvignon Blanc. That's perfectly okay. Just remember that you might need to adjust the acidity or saltiness of the salad to account for the difference in the Pinot Noir's profile. As a rule, we recommend tasting the wine, then tasting the dish, then going back and tasting the wine again. If the wine seems dull and flat, add a little more sweetness or umami to the food. If it's too tart, bring up the acid level in the food and add a little salt. If the wine remains unchanged, you've set the stage for enjoyment.

SEASONAL RECIPES

Peach Caprese Salad

*Here is Chef Kolin Vazzoler's take on insalata caprese, with seasonal, ripe peaches taking
the place of traditional tomatoes. You can use white (more floral) or yellow (more fruity)
peaches here, and for a twist—as long as they're not too ripe—try grilling them for a slightly
smoky flavor. The acid of our dry rosé counters the creamy umami taste of the mozzarella,
while the stone fruit characteristics of the wine echo the flavors of the peaches.*

2 cups sliced ripe peaches (about 3 peaches)
1 cup fresh mozzarella bocconcini (small balls)
   or cut-up larger mozzarella cheese balls
½ cup chopped roasted Marcona almonds
Leaves from 1 bunch basil, torn in half
2 tablespoons white balsamic vinegar
1 tablespoon extra-virgin olive oil
½ teaspoon fleur de sel

In a bowl, combine the peaches, mozzarella, almonds, and basil and toss to mix. Drizzle with the vinegar and olive oil, sprinkle with the fleur de sel, and toss gently to coat evenly. Divide among four small bowls or salad plates and serve.

 WINE: *SIMI Sonoma County Dry Rosé*

Lobster, Corn and Poblano Chowder

SERVES: 6

This brightly colored soup can be made quickly and served as a main course on its own.
The key components of pancetta, wine, and cream create an exquisitely balanced dish that
is an effortless match for our Russian River Valley Chardonnay Reserve. The poblano chile
adds interest but is relatively mild, so it will not interfere with the wine.

1 or 2 live lobsters (2½ to 3 pounds total)
4 cups organic chicken stock
2 ears corn, husks and silk removed
4 tablespoons extra-virgin olive oil
3 slices pancetta or bacon, cut into
small pieces
3 cloves garlic, minced
2 large yellow onions, minced
3 celery stalks, diced
½ cup SIMI Russian River Valley
Chardonnay, divided
6 tomatillos, husks removed, rinsed,
and diced
2 large Yukon Gold potatoes, peeled
and diced
2 fresh thyme sprigs
1 poblano chile, stem, seeds, and ribs
removed, diced
½ cup heavy cream
Kosher salt and freshly ground black
pepper
Small fresh flat-leaf parsley sprigs,
for garnish

Fill a large pot two-thirds full with water and bring to a rolling boil over high heat. Drop in the lobster(s) headfirst, cover the pot, and when the water returns to a boil, adjust the heat to maintain a gentle boil and start timing. Plan on 6 to 7 minutes for a 1-pound lobster, 8 to 10 minutes for a 1½-pound lobster, and 11 to 12 minutes for a 2-pound lobster. The shell of a lobster will turn red when the lobster is ready. Using tongs or a large wire skimmer, carefully remove the lobster(s) from the pot and set aside until cool enough to handle.

To remove the meat from a lobster, twist off the claws from the body, then crack each claw with a mallet or lobster cracker and pull away the shells, being careful not to tear the meat. Set the meat and shells aside separately. Next, separate the tail from the body by twisting them in opposite directions and then set the body aside. To remove the meat from the tail, snap off the flippers from the narrow end and, using a small fork or similar tool (or your finger), push the meat out the broad end. Set the tail meat aside with the claw meat, and set the tail shell aside with the claw shells. Tug at the legs and body to separate them from the back shell and set the back shell aside with the other shells. Remove the legs from the body, then remove the spongy gills, sand sac, and black vein from the body and discard. Pick out the rib meat from the body and the meat from the legs and refrigerate for another use. Cut the tail and claw meat into roughly ½-inch pieces, place in a bowl, cover, and refrigerate until serving. Gather up all of the shells and use to make the stock.

Preheat the oven to 350°F. Spread the shells on a sheet pan and roast in the oven for 15 minutes. Transfer the shells to a small stockpot, add the chicken stock, and bring to a boil over medium-high heat. Lower the heat to medium-low, cover the pot, and simmer for 45 minutes. Strain the liquid through a cheesecloth-lined sieve into a bowl and discard the shells. Set the stock aside.

(continued next page)

Hold an ear of corn stem end down in a wide, shallow bowl. Using a sharp knife, cut downward between the cob and the base of the kernels to remove the kernels but not their fibrous bases, rotating the ear after each cut. When all of the kernels have been removed, run the back of the knife down the cob to release any corn "milk" trapped in the bases. Repeat with the remaining ear of corn. Set the corn aside.

In a large, heavy pot, heat 2 tablespoons of the olive oil over medium heat. Add the pancetta and sauté until crispy, 5 to 7 minutes. Add the garlic, onions, and celery and cook, stirring, for 1 minute. Add ¼ cup of the wine and cook until reduced by half. Add the tomatillos, potatoes, the reserved stock, and the thyme and simmer until the potatoes are soft, about 10 minutes. Add the corn, chile, and cream and season with salt and pepper. Simmer to cook the corn and blend the flavors, about 3 minutes. Remove and discard the thyme and keep the soup warm.

To serve, in a sauté pan, heat the remaining 2 tablespoons olive oil over medium-low heat. Add the reserved lobster meat and sauté briefly just to heat through. Using a slotted spoon, transfer the lobster to a plate. Pour off the oil from the pan and discard, then return the pan to high heat. Add the remaining ¼ cup wine, bring to a boil, and deglaze the pan, stirring to dislodge any browned bits on the bottom. Add to the soup and taste and adjust the seasoning if needed.

Divide the lobster evenly among six warmed bowls and then ladle the hot soup into the bowls. Garnish with the parsley and serve immediately.

 WINE: *SIMI Russian River Valley Chardonnay Reserve*

Arugula, Corn, and Red Pepper Salad

SERVES: 8

This is summer at its simplest and best ... no stove required! Find the freshest corn you can for this tricolor salad. The sweet juiciness of the raw corn kernels complements the fruit-driven flavors of our Sonoma County Sauvignon Blanc, while the umami-rich cheese topping is tempered by the vinaigrette, keeping the wine's crisp acidity from becoming too strong. Delicious!

1 red bell pepper
2 ears corn, husks and silk removed
4 ounces young, tender arugula leaves
3 tablespoons extra-virgin olive oil
1 tablespoon white wine vinegar
Kosher salt and freshly ground black pepper
⅓ to ⅔ cup grated Parmesan or aged
  Asiago cheese

Stem, halve, and seed the bell pepper, then cut away the white ribs. Cut the pepper into fine julienne and transfer to a bowl.

Hold an ear of corn stem end down in a wide, shallow bowl. Using a sharp knife, cut downward between the cob and the base of the kernels to remove the kernels but not their fibrous bases, rotating the ear after each cut. Repeat with the remaining ear of corn.

Add the corn kernels and arugula to the bell pepper and toss to mix. In a small bowl, whisk together the olive oil and vinegar to make a vinaigrette and season with salt and pepper. Drizzle half of the vinaigrette over the salad and toss to coat evenly. Taste the salad and add more vinaigrette as needed. (You may not need all of it.)

Divide the salad among eight individual plates and garnish each serving with some cheese and a grind or two of pepper. Serve immediately.

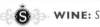 **WINE:** *SIMI Sonoma County Sauvignon Blanc*

Slow-Roasted Salmon with Cabbage and Red Wine Butter Sauce

This three-component dish deftly balances the tastes of umami, salty, sweet, and sour. With complex flavors such as earthy cabbage, caraway seeds, rosemary, and fish stock, it makes a fascinating accompaniment to the intriguing dark fruit and notes of earth and spice in our Russian River Valley Pinot Noir Reserve. We like to serve this dish on warm summer evenings at the winery on our Landslide Terrace.

CABBAGE COMPOTE

4 tablespoons unsalted butter

1 cup minced yellow onion

1 (3-pound) head savoy cabbage, cored, halved, and thinly sliced

4 ounces pancetta or prosciutto, cut into small dice

1½ cups organic chicken stock

½ cup SIMI Sonoma County Sauvignon Blanc

1 teaspoon minced fresh rosemary

1 tablespoon caraway seeds

1 Fuji apple, peeled, cored, and diced

4 (5-ounce) skinless wild salmon fillets

Kosher salt and freshly ground black pepper

RED WINE BUTTER SAUCE

½ cup Simi Russian River Valley Pinot Noir Reserve

½ cup bottled clam juice

½ cup fish stock (or additional clam juice)

1 tablespoon minced shallot

2 fresh thyme sprigs

1 bay leaf

¼ cup heavy cream

6 tablespoons unsalted butter, cut into small cubes

Kosher salt

½ teaspoon finely sliced fresh chives

To make the compote, in a large sauté pan, melt the butter over medium heat. Add the onion and sauté until translucent, about 3 minutes. Add the cabbage, pancetta, stock, wine, rosemary, and caraway seeds and stir to mix. (You may need to let the cabbage wilt a bit before you can mix in the other ingredients.) Adjust the heat to maintain a gentle simmer, cover, and cook until the liquid has nearly evaporated and the cabbage is thoroughly wilted, 20 to 30 minutes. Add the apple about 5 minutes before the compote is ready. Keep warm.

While the compote is cooking, roast the salmon. Preheat the oven to 250°F. Season the salmon on both sides with salt and pepper and arrange in a single layer in a baking dish. Roast until opaque on the outside and slightly translucent and pinkish in the center, about 25 minutes. The timing will depend on the thickness of the pieces.

To make the butter sauce, in a saucepan, combine the wine, clam juice, stock, shallot, thyme, and bay, bring to a boil over medium-high heat, and boil until the mixture is reduced by two-thirds. Pour in the cream, return to a boil, and then lower the heat to a simmer. Whisk in the butter, a cube at time, whisking after each addition until fully incorporated. When all of the butter has been added, season with salt and pour through a fine-mesh sieve placed over a bowl or measuring pitcher. The sauce is best when served immediately, but if you must hold it for a short time, keep it warm by resting it over (not touching) hot water in a larger bowl or transfer it to a thermos. Add the chives just before serving.

To serve, using a slotted spoon, divide the compote among four warmed dinner plates. Place a piece of salmon atop each serving of compote and drizzle the sauce over the top.

 WINE: *SIMI Russian River Valley Pinot Noir Reserve*

Steak Salad with Blue Cheese Dressing

SERVES: 4 to 6

Some wines simply call for a good steak. SIMI's Landslide Vineyard Cabernet Sauvignon is one of them. Umami-laden blue cheese can make a Cabernet's tannins seem too strong, which is why the addition of vinegar and sour cream—ingredients that lessen the impression of umami—to the dressing is so important here. For those who love their Cabernet all summer long, this salad is just the ticket.

BLUE CHEESE DRESSING

**4 ounces blue cheese, such as Rogue
   Creamery or Cashel**
1 cup light sour cream
2 tablespoons chopped fresh chives
1 tablespoon white wine vinegar

**2 New York steaks, about 1½ inches thick,
   trimmed of excess fat (about 1½ pounds
   total before trimming)**
1 or 2 large yellow onions, thinly sliced
All-purpose flour, for dredging
Kosher salt and freshly ground black pepper
Grapeseed oil, for deep-frying
**6 large handfuls of mixed salad greens (arugula
   and watercress are good additions)**
Chopped fresh chives, for garnish (optional)

To make the dressing, in a food processor, combine the cheese, sour cream, chives, and vinegar and process until smooth. Transfer to a bowl and set aside until serving.

Prepare a hot fire in a charcoal or gas grill for direct-heat cooking, or preheat the broiler. Leave the steaks at room temperature while the grill or broiler heats.

Separate the onion slices into rings. Place a generous layer of flour in a bowl, season with salt and pepper, and stir to mix. Pour the oil to a depth of about 3 inches into a deep, heavy saucepan and heat to 375°F. Line a sheet pan with paper towels. Preheat the oven to 200°F.

Toss the onion rings in the flour, coating them evenly and tapping off the excess, and set aside on a platter. When the oil is ready, working in small batches to avoid crowding, add the onions and fry until light brown, about 2 minutes. Using a wire skimmer, transfer to the paper towel–lined sheet pan and salt lightly. Place in the oven to keep warm until ready to serve.

Sprinkle the steaks generously on both sides with salt and pepper. If grilling the steaks, oil the grill grate; if broiling the steaks, place the steaks on a broiler pan. Place the steaks on the grill grate directly over the fire or slip them under the broiler. Cook the steaks, turning them once, until well browned on both sides, 4 to 5 minutes on each side for rare, 5 to 6 minutes for medium-rare, 6 to 7 minutes for medium, or until done to your liking. Transfer the steaks to a cutting board, tent loosely with aluminum foil, and let rest for 5 minutes.

To serve, divide the salad greens evenly among four to six dinner plates. Thinly slice the steaks against the grain and arrange the slices on the greens. Top with the dressing and a handful of the fried onion rings. Garnish with the chives, if desired, and serve immediately.

 WINE: *SIMI Landslide Vineyard Cabernet Sauvignon*

Bacon Tater Tots

This lighthearted and decadent take on tater tots still has visitors asking if we serve those "delicious tater tot things!" They are memorable, to say the least, and the nice thing about this recipe is that you can freeze some of the tots for serving at a later date.

6 ounces bacon, finely chopped

1½ pounds frozen Ore-Ida shredded hash browns, thawed and squeezed dry

½ large yellow onion, grated

2 eggs, lightly beaten

3 ounces whole-milk mozzarella or other good melting cheese, shredded (about ¾ cup)

¼ cup all-purpose flour

1 tablespoon kosher salt

1 teaspoon freshly ground black pepper

½ teaspoon Ball brand Fruit-Fresh Produce Protector (if not serving right away)

Rice bran oil, for frying

In a large frying pan, fry the bacon over medium heat until cooked but not crisp, 5 to 6 minutes. Remove the pan from the heat and let the bacon and bacon fat cool to room temperature.

Have ready one large or two smaller sheet pans. Put the potatoes in a large bowl, add the cooled bacon and bacon fat, onion, eggs, cheese, flour, salt, pepper, and produce protector, and stir gently until well mixed. Using your hands, shape the mixture into small thumb-size balls and place them, not touching, on the sheet pan(s). Refrigerate the balls until you are ready to fry them or cover and refrigerate for up to 4 hours. Alternatively, freeze the balls on the sheet pan(s), transfer to one or more airtight containers, store in the freezer for up to 1 week, and then deep-fry directly from the freezer.

Pour the oil to a depth of about 3 inches into a deep, heavy saucepan and heat to 375°F. Line a sheet pan with paper towels and place it near the stove. Preheat the oven to 200°F. Working in small batches to avoid crowding, fry the potato balls until golden brown, about 3 minutes. Using a slotted spoon, transfer the balls to the paper towel–lined sheet pan and keep warm in the oven until ready to serve. Serve the tater tots piping hot.

 WINE: *SIMI Russian River Valley Pinot Noir Reserve*

Strawberry-Rhubarb Crostata

SERVES: 6 to 8

For this summertime crostata, or tart, the pastry is shaped on a sheet pan rather than in a tart pan. It's a rustic and mouthwatering dessert—much easier to make than its more precise cousins—and the perfect host to the bountiful fruits of summer. In this version, we feature the classic combination of strawberry and rhubarb, creating a sweet-sour dynamic that pairs seamlessly with the forward fruit and crisp acidity of our dry rosé.

PASTRY DOUGH

1¼ cups all-purpose flour
1½ teaspoons granulated sugar
½ teaspoon kosher salt
½ cup cold unsalted butter, cut into small cubes
4 to 6 tablespoons ice water

FRANGIPANE

6 tablespoons unsalted butter, at room temperature
⅔ cup granulated sugar
¾ cup almond paste, at room temperature
2 teaspoons all-purpose flour
1 teaspoon cornstarch
1 whole egg plus 1 egg white
1 teaspoon vanilla extract

FILLING

2 cups strawberries, hulled and halved
1 cup sliced rhubarb, in ½-inch pieces
2 teaspoons finely grated orange zest
3 tablespoons granulated sugar
1 tablespoon cornstarch

1 egg yolk
2 tablespoons heavy cream
2 tablespoons turbinado sugar

To make the dough, in a food processor, combine the flour, granulated sugar, and salt and pulse a few times to mix. Scatter the butter over the flour mixture and pulse until some of the butter is blended with the flour and the remainder is the size of small peas (about 10 pulses). Drizzle 4 tablespoons of the ice water over the flour mixture and pulse until the dough comes together in a rough mass. To test if the dough is moist enough, squeeze a little of it in one hand; if it holds together, it is ready; if it crumbles, drizzle in a little more of the ice water and pulse just a few times to mix.

Lightly flour a work surface and transfer the dough to the floured surface. Knead lightly, shaping the dough into a thick disk. Be careful not to overmix or the pastry will be tough. Wrap the disk in plastic wrap and refrigerate for 1 hour.

Line a sheet pan with parchment paper. Clean the work surface, dust again with flour, and return the chilled dough to the floured surface. Roll out into a 12-inch round. Carefully transfer the round to the prepared sheet pan and return the dough to the refrigerator for 1 hour.

While the dough is chilling, make the frangipane. In a stand mixer fitted with the paddle attachment, or in a bowl with a handheld mixer, beat together the butter and sugar on medium-high speed until smooth. Add the almond paste and continue to beat until incorporated. Add the flour and cornstarch and then the whole egg and the egg white, beating after each addition until incorporated. Continue to beat until the mixture is very smooth. Add the vanilla extract and beat just until blended.

(continued next page)

Preheat the oven to 375°F. Remove the dough from the refrigerator. Spoon about ½ cup of the frangipane into the center of the dough. Using the back of the spoon, spread it evenly over the surface of the dough, leaving a 2-inch border uncovered. (Any unused frangipane can be transferred to an airtight container and refrigerated for up to 2 weeks.)

To make the filling, in a bowl, combine the strawberries, rhubarb, orange zest, granulated sugar, and cornstarch and stir to mix. Let sit for 5 minutes to macerate. Arrange the fruit mixture on top of the frangipane. Carefully fold the pastry border up over the fruit mixture, creating loose pleats, overlapping the edges as required, and leaving the center of the crostata open.

In a small bowl, using a fork, stir together the egg yolk and cream until blended to make an egg wash. Using a pastry brush, lightly coat the pleated edges of the crostata with the egg wash, then immediately sprinkle the turbinado sugar over the coated edges.

Bake the crostata until the crust is light golden brown and the fruit is light golden and bubbly, 40 to 50 minutes. Let cool on a wire rack for 10 to 15 minutes, then, using a wide spatula, carefully slide the crostata onto a serving plate. Cut into wedges and serve warm.

 WINE: *SIMI Sonoma County Dry Rosé*

Goat Cheese Crostini with Apples, Pistachios, Crystallized Ginger, and Chamomile Syrup

Goat cheese is fairly acidic and combining it with the mouthwatering crispness of the Granny Smith apple makes a palate-pleasing counterpoint to the sweetness in the crystallized ginger and chamomile syrup. The overall balance of this simple appetizer leaves our Sonoma County Sauvignon Blanc as crisp, fresh, and fruit-driven as our winemaker intended.

CHAMOMILE SYRUP
½ cup sugar
½ cup water
1 chamomile tea bag

1 baguette, cut on the diagonal into
  ¼-inch-thick slices
Extra-virgin olive oil, for brushing
Kosher salt and freshly ground black pepper
8 ounces fresh goat cheese
½ Granny Smith apple, cored and sliced
  paper-thin (preferably on a mandoline)
2 tablespoons chopped crystallized ginger
¼ cup chopped toasted pistachios

Preheat the oven to 350°F.

To make the syrup, in a small saucepan, combine the sugar and water and bring to a boil over high heat, stirring to dissolve the sugar. Remove from the heat, add the tea bag, and steep for 3 minutes. Remove the bag and let the syrup cool.

Arrange the baguette slices in a single layer on a sheet pan. Brush with the olive oil and sprinkle very lightly with salt and pepper. Toast in the oven until light golden and slightly crispy, about 5 minutes. Remove from the oven and let cool completely.

Spread each toast with some goat cheese and top with a few apple slices, a pinch of ginger, and a scattering of pistachios. Drizzle each toast with a little of the syrup and serve.

 WINE: *SIMI Sonoma County Sauvignon Blanc*

Oysters with Shiso Granita

Fresh shiso, which has characteristics of both basil and mint, can be found in most Asian markets, as can yuzu juice, which has a tart flavor with hints of lemon and floral orange blossom. SIMI 1876 Sparkling Wine is the classic partner to oysters for good reason, but the refreshing acidity of the Sonoma County Sauvignon Blanc works just as nicely.

2 cups water

1 cup sugar

1 tablespoon finely grated lemon zest

14 fresh shiso leaves (or large fresh basil leaves)

2 tablespoons yuzu juice

18 small oysters (such as Kumamoto, shigoku, or kusshi)

Rock salt or coarse sea salt, for serving (optional)

In a small saucepan, combine the water, sugar, lemon zest, and 12 of the shiso leaves and bring to a boil over medium-high heat, stirring to dissolve the sugar. Remove from the heat, cover, and let steep for 20 minutes. Strain the mixture through a fine-mesh sieve placed over a shallow, flat-bottomed pan or dish. Stir in the yuzu juice. Place in the freezer for 1 hour. Pull the container out of the freezer and scrape and stir the mixture with a fork to break it up into little crystal chunks, being careful to scrape down the sides as well. Return the container to the freezer for 1 hour, then repeat the scraping and stirring. Repeat this process until the granita is a good, uniform consistency of fluffy, small crystals. Transfer the granita to an airtight container and store in the freezer until serving or up to 24 hours.

To open the oysters, working with one at a time, grasp it with your nondominant hand, preferably with a folded towel for a better grip, with the hinge end facing you and the rounded end facing away from you. Insert the tip of an oyster knife or other short, sturdy blade into the dark area on the hinge end and twist forcefully to break the hinge. Run the knife between the oyster meat and top shell to sever the adductor muscle, then remove and discard the top shell. Run the knife under the oyster to free it from the bottom shell, leaving the oyster in the cupped bottom shell. Replace the oyster in the bottom shell and set aside on a sheet pan. Repeat with the remaining oysters.

To serve, stack the remaining 2 shiso leaves, roll them up lengthwise, and cut crosswise to yield fine shreds (chiffonade). If using rock salt, arrange a bed of rock salt on each of six serving plates. Divide the oysters evenly among the plates. Top each oyster with a little shiso granita and garnish with the shiso chiffonade. Serve immediately.

 WINE: *SIMI Sonoma County Sauvignon Blanc or 1876 Sparkling Wine*

Pappardelle with Duck and Porcini Ragu

SERVES: 8

When the weather starts to turn cold, almost nothing is better for dinner than this richly flavored main course, which fills the kitchen with heavenly aromas as it slowly cooks. This is a take-off on a dish Chef Kolin Vazzoler's mother makes (he still looks forward to it when he visits), only she uses beef and pork. He prefers duck for its deep, satisfying flavor and luxurious texture. The duck and porcini ragù can be made a day in advance and reheated just before you toss it with the pasta. You can also make an extra-large batch and freeze some of it for use at a later date.

RAGÙ

1½ pounds boneless duck leg meat, cut into 1-inch chunks
1 tablespoon sweet paprika
Kosher salt and freshly ground black pepper
2 tablespoons extra-virgin olive oil
¼ large yellow onion, cut into small dice
1 carrot, peeled and cut into small dice
1 celery stalk, cut into small dice
4 ounces fresh porcini (or chanterelle) mushrooms, cut into small dice
1 clove garlic, minced
1 cup canned San Marzano tomatoes
1 cup SIMI Landslide Vineyard Cabernet Sauvignon
8 black peppercorns
1 bay leaf
8 fresh flat-leaf parsley sprigs
2 fresh rosemary sprigs
2 fresh thyme sprigs
3 to 4 cups duck or chicken stock

1½ pounds dried pappardelle pasta
½ cup grated grana padano cheese
3 to 4 tablespoons unsalted butter

To make the ragù, preheat the oven to 325°F. Sprinkle the duck pieces on all sides with the paprika, salt, and pepper. In a heavy ovenproof pot, heat the olive oil over medium-high heat. Add the duck pieces and sear, turning the pieces as needed, until golden brown on all sides, 7 to 9 minutes. Using a slotted spoon, transfer the duck to a plate and set aside.

Add the onion, carrot, celery, and mushrooms to the oil remaining in the pot and cook, stirring often with a wooden spoon, until the onion is translucent, about 3 minutes. Return the duck to the pot, add the garlic, and cook, stirring, for another 1 minute. Add the tomatoes, breaking them up with the spoon, and cook, stirring occasionally, for 4 minutes. Pour in the wine and deglaze the pan, stirring to dislodge any browned bits on the bottom. Cook until the wine is reduced by half.

Put the peppercorns, bay leaf, and parsley, rosemary, and thyme sprigs on a square of cheesecloth, bring the corners together, and tie securely with kitchen string to make a pouch. Add the pouch to the pot, then pour in enough stock almost to cover the meat. Bring to a simmer, cover, transfer to the oven, and cook until the duck meat falls apart when nudged with the wooden spoon and the mixture is the consistency of a thick tomato sauce, about 2 hours. If the sauce is not thick enough, return the pot to the stove top over medium-low heat and cook uncovered until the sauce reduces and thickens. Season with salt and pepper.

To cook the pasta, bring a large pot filled with salted water to a boil over high heat. Add the pasta, stir, and cook until al dente, 8 to 10 minutes or according to package directions. Be careful not to overcook the pasta as it will cook a bit longer with the sauce.

Have the pot with the ragù on the stove top over low heat. When the pasta is ready, drain and add to the ragù with about half of the cheese and all of the butter. Stir and toss together until the pasta absorbs a little of the sauce and the sauce thickens slightly from the starch present in the pasta. Taste and adjust the seasoning with salt and pepper.

Transfer the pasta to a warmed serving bowl or individual warmed pasta bowls and top with the remaining cheese. Serve immediately.

 WINE: *SIMI Landslide Vineyard Cabernet Sauvignon*

Pan-Roasted Quail Stuffed with Mushrooms Over Polenta, Swiss Chard, and Acorn Squash

This is a special-occasion dish that richly rewards the effort that goes into it. Quail is a delicate-tasting game bird, with a flavor that is heightened by the golden chanterelles and the buttery polenta. The slightly gamy flavor of the quail and the earthiness of the mushrooms and acorn squash are mirrored in our Russian River Valley Pinot Noir Reserve, which carries hints of smoke, bacon, sage, and fir along with bright red fruit and balanced acidity.

MUSHROOM STUFFING

2 tablespoons unsalted butter
½ large white onion, minced
1 clove garlic, minced
2 pounds chanterelle or other flavorful wild
   or cultivated mushrooms, sliced
1 fresh thyme sprig
2 tablespoons SIMI Russian River Valley
   Pinot Noir Reserve
1 tablespoon chopped fresh chives
1 teaspoon chopped fresh flat-leaf parsley
Pinch of kosher salt
Pinch of freshly ground black pepper

POLENTA

4½ cups water
1 teaspoon kosher salt
1 cup polenta
3 tablespoons unsalted butter
½ cup grated pecorino romano cheese
Kosher salt and freshly ground black pepper

QUAIL

8 semiboneless quail
Pinch of kosher salt
Pinch of freshly ground black pepper
4 tablespoons olive oil
½ large yellow onion, minced
2 cloves garlic, minced
3 tablespoons brandy
1 fresh thyme sprig
¼ cup SIMI Russian River Valley
   Pinot Noir Reserve
¼ cup organic chicken stock
Kosher salt and freshly ground black pepper
1 tablespoon chopped fresh flat-leaf parsley

SQUASH AND CHARD

2 tablespoons extra-virgin olive oil
1 acorn squash, peeled, halved, seeded, and
   cut into ½-inch cubes
½ medium red onion, minced
2 bunches Swiss chard, stems and ribs
   removed and leaves cut into 1-inch pieces
Kosher salt and freshly ground black pepper

(continued next page)

To prepare the stuffing, in a sauté pan, melt the butter over medium heat. Add the onion and garlic and sauté until translucent, about 5 minutes. Add the mushrooms, thyme, and wine and sauté until the mushrooms are tender, about 5 minutes. Add the chives and parsley, season with the salt and pepper, and stir well. Remove from the heat, remove and discard the thyme sprig, and set aside.

To make the polenta, bring the water to a boil in a saucepan. Add the salt and then slowly add the polenta in a very thin, steady stream while whisking constantly. Turn the heat to medium-low and cook, whisking every couple of minutes, until the polenta is thick and pulls away from the sides of the pan, 40 to 45 minutes. Stir in the butter and cheese, season with salt and pepper, and remove from the heat. Cover to keep warm.

While the polenta is cooking, begin preparing the quail. Preheat the oven to 400°F. Open the cavity of a quail and season the cavity with some of the salt and pepper. Using a paring knife, make a ½-inch-wide slit through the right thigh near the bone. Generously stuff the cavity with the mushroom mixture, then push the left leg through the slit in the right thigh as far as it will go. This will close up the cavity and prevent the stuffing from falling out. Season the quail on all sides with salt and pepper. Repeat with the remaining quail.

Select an ovenproof sauté pan or frying pan that will accommodate all of the quail without crowding and place over medium-high heat. When the pan is quite hot, add 3 tablespoons of the olive oil and swirl the pan to coat the bottom. When the oil is hot, place the quail, breast side down, in the pan and sauté until golden brown, about

5 minutes. Flip the birds over, transfer the pan to the oven, and cook until an instant-read thermometer inserted into a thigh reads 155°F, about 10 minutes. Transfer the quail to a platter and cover with aluminum foil to keep warm.

Pour off any excess fat from the pan, return the pan to the stove top over medium-high heat, and add the remaining 1 tablespoon olive oil. When the oil is hot, add the onion and garlic and sauté until the garlic starts to turn golden, about 1 minute. Add the brandy, light a long match, and hold it just above the contents of the pan to ignite the fumes. When the flames subside, add the thyme and the Pinot Noir and cook until the liquid is reduced by half. Add the stock, bring to a boil, and season with salt and pepper. Strain through a fine-mesh sieve into a small warmed pitcher, add the parsley, and cover to keep warm.

While the quail are roasting, prepare the squash and chard. In a large sauté pan or frying pan, heat the olive oil over medium-high heat. Add the squash and cook, stirring often, until soft but not mushy, about 5 minutes. Using a slotted spoon, transfer the squash to a plate and keep warm. Add the red onion to the pan and cook, stirring, for 1 minute. Add the chard and cook, stirring and tossing, until wilted, about 3 minutes. Return the squash to the pan, stir to mix, and season with salt and pepper.

To serve, place a large spoonful of polenta onto the center of each warmed dinner plate. Top the polenta with the squash and chard and crown with a quail. Drizzle with the sauce and serve immediately.

 WINE: *SIMI Russian River Valley Pinot Noir Reserve*

Brussels Sprouts with Crispy Lamb Belly

SERVES: 4

Like pork belly, lamb belly is an increasingly popular ingredient and can be found in specialty stores, particularly in urban areas (if lamb belly is unavailable where you live, you can substitute pancetta or even bacon). A flavorful, fatty cut, lamb belly (also known as lamb breast) is easy to cure and makes a mouthwatering accompaniment to the crispy Brussels sprout leaves in this recipe. Caramelizing the Brussels sprouts make these otherwise sulfurous vegetables a fine match for our Alexander Valley Cabernet Sauvignon.

CURED LAMB BELLY
½ **cup kosher salt**
2 **tablespoons maple sugar**
2 **tablespoons very finely chopped fresh**
   rosemary
1½ **tablespoons fennel pollen**
¾ **teaspoon black peppercorns**
¾ **teaspoon freshly grated nutmeg**
¾ **teaspoon red pepper flakes**
2 **large cloves garlic, minced**
1 **(1-pound) piece lamb belly**

1 **pound Brussels sprouts**
1 **tablespoon extra-virgin olive oil**
1 **tablespoon unsalted butter**
Kosher salt and freshly ground black pepper
Finely grated zest and juice of 1 lemon

To cure the lamb belly, in a small bowl, combine the salt, maple sugar, rosemary, fennel pollen, peppercorns, nutmeg, red pepper flakes, and garlic and stir to mix well. Spread the salt mixture evenly over the lamb belly and place the belly in a shallow container. Cover and refrigerate for 2 days.

Rinse the spice mixture off the lamb belly and pat dry. Cut the lamb belly in half crosswise and reserve half of the belly for another use. It will keep tightly wrapped in the refrigerator for up to 2 weeks. Slice the remaining half crosswise into 1/2-inch-thick slices.

To prepare the Brussels sprouts, working with one at a time, insert the tip of a small, sharp paring knife or a vegetable peeler alongside the stem and twist the knife or peeler to release the core from the sprout; separate the leaves with your fingers. Repeat with the remaining sprouts.

In a large frying pan, heat the olive oil and butter over medium-high heat. When the fat is hot, add the belly slices and sauté, turning as needed, until browned on both sides. Transfer to a plate and keep warm. Add the Brussels sprout leaves to the pan and fry, stirring occasionally, until crispy, about 3 minutes. Season with salt and pepper and the lemon zest. Return the lamb to the pan and mix gently.

Transfer the contents of the pan to a serving dish and finish with a drizzle of lemon juice for a touch of acidity. Serve immediately.

 WINE: *SIMI Alexander Valley Cabernet Sauvignon*

Persimmon Pudding with Crème Anglaise and Cranberry Compote

SERVES: 8

Chef Kolin Vazzoler learned how to make this dish while working with Chef Gary Danko at Danko's eponymous Michelin-rated restaurant in San Francisco. It's important to use acorn-shaped Hachiya persimmons for this pudding (not squat Fuyus) and to make sure they're very ripe—almost overripe. This is another dessert that works with wine because it's not overly sweet. The cranberry compote brings tartness and acidity to the dish, and the spices in the pudding marry nicely with the hints of gingerbread in the Russian River Valley Pinot Noir Reserve.

CRANBERRY COMPOTE

1 ½ teaspoons powdered gelatin
⅓ cup apple juice
1 pound cranberries
1 cup granulated sugar
⅓ cup fresh orange juice
¼ cup SIMI Russian River Valley
  Pinot Noir Reserve
3 tablespoons fresh lime juice
Pinch of kosher salt

PERSIMMON PUDDING

1 ½ cups all-purpose flour
1 teaspoon freshly ground cinnamon
1 teaspoon freshly grated nutmeg
1 teaspoon baking soda
½ teaspoon kosher salt
2 cups persimmon puree (from 4 to 5
  Hachiya persimmons)
2 eggs
1 cup firmly packed light brown sugar
½ cup unsalted butter, melted
1 teaspoon vanilla extract
1 cup light cream or half-and-half

CRÈME ANGLAISE

4 egg yolks
¼ cup granulated sugar
Pinch of salt
1 cup light cream or half-and-half
½ vanilla bean

2 Fuyu persimmons, sliced crosswise
  paper-thin, for garnish (optional)
8 small fresh mint sprigs, for garnish
  (optional)

To make the compote, in a small bowl, sprinkle the gelatin over the apple juice and let sit for 5 minutes. In a saucepan, combine the cranberries, granulated sugar, orange juice, wine, lime juice, salt, and gelatin mixture and place over medium heat. Bring just to a simmer, reduce the heat to medium-low and cook, stirring, until the berries begin to pop but are still whole, 5 to 7 minutes. Then immediately remove from the heat and let cool. (Do not allow the mixture to boil or the gelatin will lose its setting ability.) Transfer to an airtight container and refrigerate until set, at least 2 hours. (You will have more compote than you will need. Any remaining compote will keep for up to 1 month.)

(continued next page)

To make the persimmon pudding, preheat the oven to 350°F. Butter one 9-by-3-inch round cake pan or springform pan (with a tight seal) or eight ½-cup molds (plain or fluted) or ramekins.

In a bowl, sift together the flour, cinnamon, nutmeg, baking soda, and salt. In a separate bowl, whisk together the persimmon puree, eggs, brown sugar, butter, vanilla extract, and cream. Add the flour mixture to the persimmon mixture and whisk just until well mixed. Pour the batter into the prepared pan or divide evenly among the prepared molds. Cover tightly with aluminum foil, shiny side down.

Place the pan or the molds (not touching) in a baking pan. Pour water into the baking pan to come about halfway up the sides of the cake pan or the molds. Bake until a skewer inserted into the center of the pudding comes out clean, 2 to 2½ hours for the cake pan or 45 minutes for the molds.

While the pudding is baking, make the crème anglaise. In a heavy saucepan, whisk together the egg yolks, granulated sugar, and salt until well blended. Set aside. Prepare an ice bath in a large bowl and set a medium bowl in the ice bath.

In a small saucepan, heat the cream over medium heat just to a boil. Remove from the heat. Using a sharp knife, split the vanilla bean lengthwise, then use the tip of the knife to scrape the vanilla seeds into the hot cream. Infuse the cream for several minutes, stirring constantly.

Gradually add the hot cream to the egg mixture while whisking constantly. Place the pan over medium-low heat and cook, stirring constantly but gently, until the custard coats the back of a spoon, 4 to 5 minutes. Do not allow the custard to boil.

Remove from the heat, stir gently once or twice until smooth, and then strain through a fine-mesh sieve into the bowl nested in the ice bath. Let cool completely, stirring occasionally. Cover and refrigerate until serving.

When the pudding is ready, remove from the water bath and let cool on a rack until lukewarm. Run a knife along the inside edge of the large pan or of the individual molds to loosen the pudding. If using a cake pan, invert the pan onto the rack, lift off the pan, and turn the pudding right side up on a serving plate. If using a springform pan, unclasp and remove the pan sides and slide the pudding onto a serving plate. If using individual molds, wait to unmold until serving.

To serve, spoon the crème anglaise onto eight individual serving plates. Divide the Fuyu persimmon slices evenly among the plates, arranging them on the crème anglaise. If you have baked a single large pudding, cut it into wedges and place a wedge atop the persimmon slices on each plate. If using individual molds, carefully invert a pudding onto each plate. Finish each plate with a spoonful of the compote, placing it next to the pudding, and garnish with a mint sprig, if desired.

 WINE: *SIMI Russian River Valley Pinot Noir Reserve*

Belgian Endive and Dungeness Crab Salad

SERVES: 6

In Northern California, the onset of winter means that Dungeness crab season is under way. It's a cause for celebration, as it doesn't last long. For many California families, serving Dungeness crab on Christmas Eve is a cherished holiday tradition. In this dish, the tender, sweet flesh of the crab coupled with the rich avocado is enlivened by the champagne vinegar and lemon juice of the vinaigrette. This is a perfect match for our Sonoma County Sauvignon Blanc, with the wine's flavors echoed in the salad's notes of fresh herbs and red pepper.

VINAIGRETTE

2 tablespoons fresh lemon juice
2 tablespoons champagne vinegar
½ teaspoon Dijon mustard
½ shallot, minced
Pinch of kosher salt
Pinch of freshly ground black pepper
⅔ cup extra-virgin olive oil

8 heads Belgian endive, leaves separated
 and torn in half, covered with a damp
 towel, and well chilled
6 ounces fresh-cooked Dungeness crabmeat,
 picked over for bits of shell and cartilage
½ red bell pepper, seeds and white ribs
 removed and cut into small dice
½ ripe avocado, peeled and cut into
 small dice
2 teaspoons chopped fresh basil
1 teaspoon chopped fresh chives
½ teaspoon chopped fresh flat-leaf parsley
Kosher salt and freshly ground black pepper

To make the vinaigrette, in a small bowl, whisk together the lemon juice, vinegar, mustard, shallot, salt, and pepper. Slowly whisk in the olive oil until emulsified. Set aside.

In a large bowl, combine the endive, crabmeat, bell pepper, avocado, basil, chives, and parsley. Drizzle about two-thirds of the vinaigrette over the salad and toss gently to coat evenly, adding more vinaigrette as needed. Season with salt and pepper. Divide the salad among six individual plates. Serve immediately.

 WINE: *SIMI Sonoma County Sauvignon Blanc*

Citrus-Cured Salmon with Meyer Lemon Radish

Curing your own salmon is not difficult, and nothing beats its ocean-infused fresh flavor. Meyer lemons, which are not as tart as regular lemons, are common in California and other warm regions, but if you don't have access to them, use a combination of juice from regular lemons mixed with a little orange juice for seasoning the salmon. The oily richness of the cured salmon makes it a good partner for the full-bodied texture of our Russian River Valley Chardonnay Reserve.

¼ cup plus 2 tablespoons kosher salt

¼ cup sugar

I bunch dill, chopped

Finely grated zest of I orange

Finely grated zest and juice of 2 Meyer lemons, plus I whole Meyer lemon for plating

I tablespoon Dijon mustard

I filleted half side salmon (not the tail end) with skin intact, pin bones removed (about 2 pounds)

3 red radishes, shaved paper-thin on a mandoline or with a sharp knife

Toasted brioche slices and crème fraîche, for serving (optional)

In a small bowl, combine the salt, sugar, dill, orange zest, lemon zest and juice, and mustard and mix well. In a large, rectangular pan that will accommodate the salmon flat, spread half of the salt mixture to about the dimension of the salmon and lay the salmon, skin side down, on the salt mixture. Spread the remaining salt mixture evenly over the surface of the salmon, cover the pan with plastic wrap, and refrigerate for 24 hours.

Rinse the cure mixture off of the salmon and pat the salmon dry. At this point, the salmon can be wrapped in plastic wrap and refrigerated for up to I week before serving.

Cut the salmon on the diagonal into thin slices, leaving the skin behind, and arrange the slices on a platter. Using a Microplane or other fine-rasp grater or a zester, grate the zest of the whole lemon evenly over the slices. Scatter the radishes over the top and serve. Accompany with the brioche slices and crème fraîche, if desired.

 WINE: *SIMI Russian River Valley Chardonnay Reserve*

Brassicas with Bagna Cauda Sauce

In Chef Kolin Vazzoler's home, this is a traditional holiday side dish served family-style as a fondue, but at the winery we present it as composed individual servings. Almost anything from the Brassica genus will work with this robustly flavored sauce. A few classics (Brussels sprouts, cauliflower) are included here along with some more unusual choices, such as small, white Tokyo turnips, watermelon radishes (a jewel-like heirloom variety that is green on the outside and red on the inside), and breakfast radishes (a red-and-white, typically oblong variety that isn't as spicy as the more common red globe radish).

1 head cauliflower, broken into florets
½ cup heavy cream
Kosher salt and freshly ground black pepper
¾ cup unsalted butter
2 tablespoons garlic-flavored olive oil
4 kale leaves, stems removed and leaves cut crosswise into 1-inch-wide strips
6 Brussels sprouts, about 1 inch long, trimmed and halved lengthwise
6 Tokyo turnips, trimmed, peeled, and blanched until crisp-tender, about 2 minutes
3 broccoli rabe stalks, tough stem ends trimmed, cut into 2-inch lengths, and blanched until crisp-tender, about 2 minutes

BAGNA CAUDA SAUCE
¾ cup extra-virgin olive oil
½ cup unsalted butter
16 cloves garlic, grated on a Microplane or other fine-rasp grater
12 olive oil–packed anchovy fillets, drained and minced
Finely grated zest and juice of 1 lemon
2 tablespoons minced fresh flat-leaf parsley

1 rutabaga, peeled and shaved paper-thin with a mandoline
1 watermelon radish, peeled and shaved paper-thin with a mandoline
3 breakfast radishes, trimmed and shaved paper-thin with a mandoline
2 tablespoons extra-virgin olive oil
Juice of ½ lemon
Assorted microgreens, such as beet greens and baby watercress, for garnish

Set half of the cauliflower florets aside. Place the other half in a saucepan, add the cream and then water to cover, and season with salt. Bring to a boil over high heat, adjust the heat to a simmer, and cook until tender but not mushy, about 5 minutes. Remove from the heat and drain, reserving the cooking liquid.

Transfer the cooked cauliflower to a blender and blend until smooth, adding some of the cooking liquid as needed to make a smooth puree. Season with salt and set aside. Keep warm.

In a large sauté pan, melt ½ cup of the butter over medium-high heat. Add the reserved cauliflower florets and panfry until golden brown and tender, about 5 minutes. Drain the florets in a sieve and then set aside on a sheet pan.

Wipe out the sauté pan, return the pan to medium-high heat, and add the garlic-flavored olive oil. When the oil is hot, add the kale and sauté until tender, about 3 minutes. Set aside on the sheet pan with the cauliflower.

(continued next page)

Wipe out the sauté pan, return the pan to medium-high heat, and add the remaining 4 tablespoons butter. When the butter melts, add the Brussels sprouts and sauté until golden brown and tender, 3 to 4 minutes. Season the sprouts with salt and set aside on the same sheet pan. Add the turnips and broccoli rabe to the sheet pan.

To make the sauce, in a saucepan, combine the olive oil, butter, garlic, and anchovies and bring to a bare simmer over medium heat. Turn the heat to the lowest setting and cook for 1 hour to soften the flavors. Check the pan frequently to make sure the heat is not too high, as the mixture can scorch easily. When ready to serve, stir in the lemon zest and juice and the parsley.

Preheat the oven to 350°F. When the oven is ready, place the sheet pan holding the vegetables in the oven until they are hot, about 4 minutes.

While the vegetables are heating, in a bowl, combine the rutabaga, watermelon radish, and breakfast radishes. Drizzle with the olive oil and lemon juice, season with salt and pepper, and toss to coat evenly.

Divide the cauliflower puree evenly among six individual serving plates. Arrange the warm vegetables and the dressed raw radishes and rutabaga on top of the puree. Stir the bagna cauda sauce briefly, then drizzle it over the vegetables. Garnish with the microgreens and serve immediately.

 **WINE:** *SIMI Sonoma County Chardonnay*

Fennel-Crusted Rack of Pork with Roasted Root Vegetables

This festive cold-weather dish is ideal for a dinner party, as most of the work can be done in advance. To save time, ask your butcher to french the rack (remove the fat, membrane, and meat from the ribs). The acidity of the brandy and wine in the pan sauce tempers the umami taste of the roasted meat and caramelized vegetables, balancing the dish for service with our Landslide Vineyard Cabernet Sauvignon. At the same time, the herb-studded crust of the rack, with its fennel, rosemary, sage, and thyme, complements the wine's compelling flavors of cherry, plum, and black pepper spice.

PORK

1 (8-pound) rack of pork, frenched
   (8-chop rack)
4 cloves garlic, sliced
1 tablespoon fresh rosemary, coarsely
   chopped
1 tablespoon dried sage
2 teaspoons fennel seeds, toasted in a dry
   pan over low heat until aromatic and
   then crushed
2 teaspoons dried thyme
Kosher salt and freshly ground black pepper
¼ cup Dijon mustard
Canola or grapeseed oil, for browning
2 tablespoons brandy
½ cup SIMI Landslide Vineyard Cabernet
   Sauvignon
1 cup organic chicken stock

ROOT VEGETABLES

8 ounces sweet potato, peeled and cut into
   1-inch pieces
8 ounces rutabaga, peeled and cut into
   1-inch pieces
8 ounces celery root, peeled and cut into
   1-inch pieces
8 ounces parsnip, peeled and cut into
   ½-inch pieces
3 cloves garlic, thinly sliced
3 fresh thyme sprigs
¼ cup plus 1 tablespoon extra-virgin olive oil
2 tablespoons maple syrup
3 teaspoons kosher salt
Freshly ground black pepper
Cayenne pepper
2 Granny Smith apples, peeled, cored, and
   cut into 1-inch pieces
1 large leek, white part only, thinly sliced
1 large fennel bulb, stems and fronds
   removed and bulb cut into wedges

GARNISH

8 ounces mâche
1 tablespoon extra-virgin olive oil
Kosher salt and freshly ground pepper

(continued next page)

To prepare the pork, using a paring knife, make ½-inch-deep incisions all over the pork and press the garlic slices into the incisions. In a small bowl, combine the rosemary, sage, fennel seeds, thyme, 1 tablespoon salt, and ½ teaspoon pepper and mix well. Using a pastry brush, coat the pork evenly with the mustard, then rub the herb mixture evenly over the pork. Cover and let sit at room temperature for 1 hour.

Preheat the oven to 450°F. Heat a large frying pan over medium-high heat. When the pan is hot, add enough oil to film the bottom lightly. Place the pork, bone side up, in the pan and cook until well browned, about 4 minutes. Turn the rack over and brown other side, 3 to 4 minutes longer. Transfer the pork, bone side up, to a sheet pan.

Add the brandy to the frying pan over medium-high heat, bring to a boil, and boil for 1 minute, stirring to dislodge any browned bits on the bottom. Add the wine and cook until reduced by half, about 5 minutes. Pour in the stock and boil until reduced by half, 6 to 8 minutes. Season with salt and pepper. Set aside off the heat.

Roast the pork for 15 minutes. Lower the oven temperature to 350°F and continue to roast the pork for 15 minutes more.

While the pork is roasting, prepare the root vegetables. In a large bowl, combine the sweet potato, rutabaga, celery root, parsnip, garlic, and thyme. In a small bowl, whisk together the ¼ cup olive oil, the maple syrup, and 2 teaspoons of the salt. Pour the oil mixture over the vegetables, season with black pepper and a pinch of cayenne, toss to coat evenly, and transfer to a roasting pan. When the pork has roasted for 15 minutes at 350°F, add the root vegetables to the same oven and continue roasting the pork and vegetables for 30 minutes longer.

While the pork and root vegetables are roasting, add the apples, leek, fennel, and the remaining 1 tablespoon olive oil and 1 teaspoon salt to the same bowl that held the root vegetables. Season with black pepper and toss to coat evenly. When the pork and root vegetables have roasted for 30 minutes, add the apple-leek mixture to the root vegetables. Continue to roast the pork until an instant-read thermometer inserted into the thickest part away from bone reads 145°F and the vegetables are tender, about 15 minutes more.

Remove the pork and the vegetables from the oven, tent the pork loosely with aluminum foil, lightly cover the vegetables with foil, and let rest for 10 minutes.

While the pork and vegetables are resting, assemble the garnish. Put the mâche in a bowl, drizzle with the olive oil, season with salt and pepper, and toss to coat evenly.

To serve, slice the pork into individual chops and pour any juices that are released into the sauce, then quickly reheat the sauce. Divide the roasted vegetables among eight warmed dinner plates. Lean a rib of pork on top of the vegetables and spoon the pan sauce on the base of the pork. Place a handful of the mâche on top of each rib bone. Serve immediately.

 WINE: SIMI Landslide Vineyard Cabernet Sauvignon

Tuscan Meatballs

MAKES 36 MEATBALLS; SERVES: 6 to 8

Comfort food at its best, this classic dish is an adaptation of the recipe Chef Kolin Vazzoler's Italian grandmother made throughout his childhood. If your butcher does not have pork fatback on hand, ask him or her to special order it for you. Look for fennel pollen in specialty food stores or online. If you have leftover meatballs, they can be frozen and warmed up as needed. These meatballs are also delicious served atop pasta or slices of grilled country bread drizzled with olive oil.

12 ounces boneless pork butt, cut into
   1-inch squares
12 ounces boneless beef short rib, cut into
   1-inch squares
3 ounces pork fatback, cut into 1-inch
   squares
3 ounces pancetta, cut into 1-inch squares
8 ounces focaccia, cut into 1-inch squares
¾ cup coarsely chopped fresh flat-leaf
   parsley
1 tablespoon fresh oregano leaves
2 teaspoons fennel pollen
1 teaspoon red pepper flakes
1 teaspoon freshly cracked black pepper
2 tablespoons kosher salt
¾ cup fresh whole-milk ricotta cheese
3 eggs, lightly beaten
¼ cup whole milk
1 (28-ounce) can San Marzano tomatoes
½ cup fresh basil leaves
Wedge of Parmigiano-Reggiano cheese,
   for serving

In a large bowl, combine the pork, beef, fatback, pancetta, focaccia, parsley, oregano, fennel pollen, red pepper flakes, black pepper, and 1 tablespoon of the salt and mix well. Cover and refrigerate for 30 minutes to chill and marinate.

Fit a meat grinder with the medium plate (die). Pass the meat mixture through the grinder, capturing the mixture in a bowl. (If you do not have a meat grinder, have your butcher grind the pork, beef, fatback, and pancetta. Place the focaccia in a food processor and pulse until finely ground. In a large bowl, combine the ground meats, focaccia, parsley, oregano, fennel pollen, red pepper flakes, black pepper, and 1 tablespoon of salt and mix just to combine.)

In second bowl, combine the ricotta, eggs, and milk and whisk until blended. Add the ricotta mixture to the meat mixture and mix lightly to combine. Cover and refrigerate for 1 hour.

Preheat the oven to 375°F. Line two sheet pans with parchment paper. Form the mixture into 36 balls 1½ to 2 inches in diameter and place them on the pans. Bake the meatballs for 15 minutes. Remove from the oven and lower the oven temperature to 275°F.

In a blender, combine the tomatoes and the remaining 1 tablespoon salt and blend just until a coarse sauce forms. Pour the sauce into a roasting pan just large enough to accommodate the meatballs in a single layer. Arrange the meatballs in the pan, making sure they are covered with the sauce. Add the basil leaves, distributing them evenly around the pan.

Cover the pan tightly with aluminum foil. Transfer to the oven and braise until the meatballs are cooked through and slightly browned and the sauce is bubbling, about 1½ hours.

Remove from the oven, grate the Parmigiano-Reggiano over the top, and serve.

 WINE: *SIMI Sonoma County Merlot*

Gingerbread with Cardamom Poached Pears

SERVES: 12

We like serving this on winter nights in our dining room at the winery, with a wood fire blazing and candles aglow. This is another dessert in which the sweetness is tempered by savory spices such as ginger and cloves, making it a fetching match for the supple tannins of our Landslide Vineyard Cabernet Sauvignon.

GINGERBREAD

1 cup sugar

1 cup unsulfured light molasses

½ cup corn oil

3 eggs

2 cups all-purpose flour

2 teaspoons baking soda

1 teaspoon ground cloves

1 teaspoon ground ginger

½ teaspoon freshly grated nutmeg

¾ teaspoon kosher salt

1 cup boiling water

POACHED PEARS

3 cups water

1 cup SIMI Sonoma County Sauvignon Blanc

1 cup sugar

2 teaspoons ground cardamom

4 whole cloves

2 cinnamon sticks

4 lemon zest strips, each 2 inches long by
   ½ inch wide

2 tablespoons fresh lemon juice

1 vanilla bean, split lengthwise

6 medium-ripe Bartlett or Comice pears,
   peeled, halved with stem intact, and cored

1 cup heavy cream

1 tablespoon sugar

To make the gingerbread, preheat the oven to 325°F. Butter one 9-by-5-inch loaf pan.

In a bowl, whisk together the sugar, molasses, corn oil, and eggs until blended. In a separate bowl, sift together the flour, baking soda, cloves, ginger, nutmeg, and salt. Add the flour mixture to the egg mixture and stir until combined. Add the boiling water and stir until well blended. Pour the batter into the prepared loaf pan.

Bake the gingerbread until a skewer inserted into the center comes out clean, 45 minutes to 1 hour. Let cool completely in the pan on a rack. To unmold, run a knife along the inside edge of the pan to loosen the gingerbread, invert the pan onto the rack, lift off the pan, and turn the gingerbread upright. The gingerbread will taste better if allowed to sit for a day before serving. It will keep well wrapped in the refrigerator for up to 2 weeks.

To poach the pears, in a large saucepan, combine the water, wine, sugar, cardamom, cloves, cinnamon sticks, lemon zest and juice, and vanilla bean and bring to a boil over medium-high heat, stirring until the sugar dissolves. Add the pears, return the liquid to a boil, adjust the heat to maintain a gentle simmer, and poach the pears just until tender when pierced with a skewer, about 20 minutes.

Remove from the heat and let cool to room temperature. Transfer the pears and their liquid to a bowl, cover tightly, and refrigerate until serving. They will keep for up to 1 week.

Just before serving, in a bowl, combine the cream and sugar and whip with an electric mixer on medium-high speed or with a whisk by hand until soft peaks form.

To serve, cut the gingerbread into slabs and place on individual dessert plates. Lean a pear half against the gingerbread and drizzle a little of the poaching liquid on the pear and the gingerbread. Place a scoop of the whipped cream alongside.

 WINE: *SIMI Landslide Vineyard Cabernet Sauvignon*

Chilled English Pea Soup with Fennel Salad

SERVES: 6

Nothing says springtime like fresh English peas, those bright green harbingers that turn up in many farmers' markets and grocery stores when the weather begins to warm. And the pods left over from shelling can be made into a lovely vegetable stock. If fresh peas aren't available in your area, frozen peas will also work nicely in this soup.

SOUP

1 tablespoon extra-virgin olive oil

1 large yellow onion, minced

4 cups shelled fresh English peas (from about 4 pounds unshelled) or frozen petite peas

3 cups vegetable stock or water

2 tablespoons heavy cream (optional)

Pinch of kosher salt

Pinch of freshly ground white pepper

1 tablespoon SIMI Sonoma County Chardonnay

SALAD

¼ fennel bulb, shaved paper-thin

¼ English cucumber, halved lengthwise, seeded, and cut into ⅛-inch-thick half-moons

12 fresh tarragon leaves, very finely sliced

½ bunch fresh chives, chopped

Pinch of kosher salt

Pinch of freshly ground black pepper

1 teaspoon fresh lemon juice

1 tablespoon extra-virgin olive oil

Small fresh fennel fronds, tarragon leaves, and pea shoots, for garnish (optional)

To make the soup, in a saucepan, warm the olive oil over medium heat. Add the onion and sauté until soft, about 3 minutes. Add the peas and stock, raise the heat to medium-high, and bring to a boil. Lower the heat to a simmer and cook for 10 minutes. The peas should be very tender.

Remove from the heat and drain into a sieve placed over a bowl. Add the contents of the sieve and about 2 cups of the liquid to a blender. Puree until smooth, adding more of the liquid as needed to achieve a smooth, fluid soup consistency. If desired, blend in the cream to enrich the soup. Season the soup with the salt, pepper, and wine.

Transfer the soup to a large pitcher, cover with plastic wrap, and refrigerate for at least 1 hour or up to 1 day before serving.

When ready to serve, make the salad. In a bowl, combine the shaved fennel, cucumber, tarragon, and chives and toss to mix well. Season with the salt and pepper, drizzle with the lemon juice and olive oil, and toss to coat evenly.

Remove the soup from the refrigerator, taste, and adjust the seasoning as needed (chilling the soup dulls its aroma and flavor). Divide the chilled soup among six individual serving bowls and place a small mound of the salad in the center of each bowl. Garnish with the fennel fronds, tarragon, and pea shoots, if desired.

 WINE: *SIMI Sonoma County Chardonnay*

Avocado Toast with Smoked Trout

The lemon and lime in this light spring appetizer are a wonderful counterpoint to the richness of the fresh avocado and smoky trout. The inherent balance of the dish makes it a good match for our Sonoma County Chardonnay, though its richer flavors also contrast nicely with the acidity of our sparkling wine. You can make the avocado mixture up to 6 hours in advance. Prepare it as directed, reserving the avocado pit, then nest the pit in the center of the finished mixture, cover the bowl tightly with plastic wrap, and refrigerate until serving.

1 ripe avocado
Juice of ¼ lemon
Juice of ¼ lime
Kosher salt and freshly cracked black pepper
1 tablespoon finely chopped fresh flat-leaf
    parsley
8 slices rustic baguette, toasted
1 smoked trout fillet, about 4 ounces,
    skinned and flaked
Extra-virgin olive oil, for drizzling

Halve and pit the avocado and, using a spoon, scoop the flesh from the skin into a bowl. Add the lemon juice and lime juice and season with salt and pepper. Using a fork, mash the ingredients together, keeping the mixture slightly chunky. Stir in the parsley, then taste and adjust the seasoning.

Spread the avocado mixture onto the baguette toasts, dividing it evenly. Top each toast with an equal amount of the trout, then drizzle with the olive oil. Serve immediately.

 WINE: *SIMI 1876 Sparkling Wine or Sonoma County Chardonnay*

Black Olive Pesto Pizzette

The star of this pesto is the humble black olive, which is mixed with garlic, pine nuts, Asiago cheese, and olive oil and then spread on flaky, easy-to-use store-bought puff pastry. This is an earthy dish, its flavors echoed in the rich fruit, green peppercorn spice, and hints of cedar and tobacco in our Landslide Vineyard Cabernet Sauvignon. You will have pesto left over, which will make a delightful topping for pasta or spread for sandwiches.

BLACK OLIVE PESTO

2¼ cups pitted Kalamata olives

2 cloves garlic

2 tablespoons pine nuts

¾ cup grated aged Asiago cheese

½ cup extra-virgin olive oil

**1 sheet frozen puff pastry, about
9 by 13 inches (about 8½ ounces),
thawed according to package directions**

Preheat the oven to 450°F. Lightly oil a sheet pan.

To make the pesto, drain the olives well, then slice half of them and leave the remainder whole. In a food processor, combine the garlic and pine nuts and pulse until finely chopped. Add the whole olives, cheese, and olive oil and process until a puree forms. Transfer to a bowl, add the sliced olives, and stir to mix.

Lay the puff pastry on the prepared sheet pan. Spread about 1½ cups of the pesto evenly over the pastry, leaving a 1-inch border uncovered around the edges. Transfer the remaining pesto to an airtight container and refrigerate for up to 5 days.

Bake until the edges of the pastry are puffed and lightly browned, 10 to 15 minutes. Cut into wedges and serve.

 WINE: *SIMI Landslide Vineyard Cabernet Sauvignon*

Roasted Beet Salad with Charred Green Onions, Avocado, Capriago, and Meyer Lemon Vinaigrette

Chef Kolin Vazzoler describes this dish as a "garden on a plate," a salad composed atop a layer of edible "dirt" made of sugar, flours, ground coffee, and butter. This visually arresting plate offers a riot of flavors and textures, the beets and smoky-charred green onions delivering an earthy contrast to the sweet-crunchy "dirt" and creamy Capriago cheese. Our Sonoma County Sauvignon Blanc, with its zesty citrus notes, crisp acidity, and understated mineral tones, is a refreshing accompaniment to this fun and multifaceted first course.

BEETS

3 red beets (about 1¼ pounds total)
3 golden beets (about 1¼ pounds total)
1 tablespoon extra-virgin olive oil

VINAIGRETTE

Finely grated zest and juice of 1 Meyer
  lemon
Finely grated zest of 1 orange
Juice of ½ orange
1 tablespoon honey
½ cup extra-virgin olive oil
Pinch of kosher salt
Pinch of freshly ground black pepper

AVOCADO PUREE

2 ripe avocados
Juice of 1 lemon
Kosher salt

GRILLED GREEN ONIONS

2 green onions
1 teaspoon extra-virgin olive oil

EDIBLE "DIRT"

⅔ cup sugar
⅔ cup almond flour
⅓ cup all-purpose flour
2 tablespoons ground dark-roast coffee
1 tablespoon kosher salt
½ cup unsalted butter, melted

3 ounces Bohemian Creamery Capriago
  cheese (semifirm goat cheese) or
  Fontina cheese, rind removed and cut
  into ½-inch cubes
Assorted microgreens, such as beet greens,
  watercress, and pea shoots, for garnish

To prepare the beets, preheat the oven to 425°F. Wipe or gently scrub the beets, being carefully not to break the skin. Trim off the leaves and the stem from each beet, leaving 1 inch of the stem intact, and leave the "tail" on. Keeping the golden beets and red beets separate, place each batch on a large sheet of aluminum foil and then drizzle each batch evenly with half of the olive oil. Bring the foil up around the beets and tightly seal the edges closed to create two neat packages.

Place the packets directly on the middle rack of the oven and roast the beets until tender, about 1 hour. Test for doneness by opening a packet enough to pierce the largest

(continued next page)

beet with a knife. If the knife enters easily, the beet is done. Remove the packets from the oven, unwrap the beets, and let them sit until cool enough to handle. Continue to keep them separate so the red beets don't bleed onto the golden beets.

Using your hands, gently rub the skins from the red beets (or use a paring knife to peel them). Cut each beet into narrow wedges and transfer to a bowl. Remove the skins from the golden beets the same way, cut the beets into narrow wedges, and place in a separate bowl. Set the beets aside until serving.

To make the vinaigrette, in a small bowl, whisk together the lemon zest and juice, orange zest and juice, and honey until blended, then whisk in the olive oil. Season with the salt and pepper, then taste and adjust the seasoning if needed. Set aside until serving.

To make the avocado puree, one at a time, halve and pit the avocados and, using a spoon, scoop the flesh from the skin into a blender. Add the lemon juice and puree until smooth. Season with salt, transfer to a squeeze bottle with a wide tip, and set aside until serving.

To grill the green onions, prepare a hot fire for direct-heat cooking in a charcoal or gas grill or preheat a ridged stove-top grill pan over high heat. Trim off the root end of each green onion and then cut off any damaged tips from the green tops. Coat the onions evenly with the olive oil. Place the onions on the grill grate directly over the fire or on the grill pan and cook, turning them as needed, until lightly charred on all sides, 2 to 3 minutes; the timing will depend on the size of the onions. Transfer to a cutting board, let cool, and cut crosswise into 1- to 2-inch pieces.

To make the "dirt," preheat the oven to 350°F (325°F if using a convection setting). In a bowl, whisk together the sugar, almond flour, all-purpose flour, coffee, and salt. Pour in the butter and stir with a wooden spoon until blended and crumbly. Spread the mixture on a sheet pan.

Bake until light golden, about 15 minutes. Remove from the oven and let cool completely. Break the dough up into rough pieces, transfer to a food processor, and pulse until reduced to the consistency of coarse sand. Transfer to a bowl, cover, and set aside until serving.

To serve, divide the vinaigrette evenly between the red and golden beets, toss gently, and let sit for 10 to 15 minutes. Arrange about 2 tablespoons of the "dirt" in a line on each individual serving plate. Using a slotted spoon, lift the beets from the vinaigrette (reserve the vinaigrette) and place the wedges randomly on top of the "dirt." Add a few of the green onion pieces and cheese cubes to each plate, again spacing them along the line of "dirt." Scatter the microgreens here and there along the line, then add dollops of the avocado puree. Drizzle some of the reserved vinaigrette over each salad and serve immediately.

 WINE: *SIMI Sonoma County Sauvignon Blanc*

Gnocchi with Spiced Tomato Fondue

One of Chef Kolin Vazzoler's fondest food memories is of the gnocchi his Italian aunt made for him as a boy, which he describes as "just like little pillows." He says that re-creating and perfecting this dish has been a "twenty-year learning process." Here, he uses Caputo 00 flour specially milled for pasta or gnocchi, a product imported from Naples, though pastry flour can be substituted. He recommends using older, less starchy potatoes to give the gnocchi a light, fluffy texture. You can use canned whole plum tomatoes (preferably San Marzano) if you don't have fresh on hand.

TOMATO FONDUE

18 plum tomatoes (about 2¼ pounds total)
¼ cup extra-virgin olive oil
1 large yellow onion, finely chopped
2 cloves garlic, crushed
1 star anise pod
½ teaspoon ground cinnamon
¼ teaspoon ground coriander
2 tablespoons sherry vinegar

GNOCCHI

2¼ pounds red potatoes
2 teaspoons kosher salt
3 eggs, beaten
1⅓ cups Caputo brand 00 flour for pasta
    or gnocchi or pastry flour
4 tablespoons unsalted butter

Grated Parmesan cheese, for serving

To make the fondue, bring a large saucepan filled with water to a rolling boil. Set a large bowl of ice-cold water nearby. Core each tomato, then cut a shallow X in the blossom end. A few at a time, plunge the tomatoes into the boiling water just until their skins begin to wrinkle, about 30 seconds. Then, using a slotted spoon, transfer the tomatoes to the cold water, let cool, peel, halve, and seed. When all of the tomatoes are peeled and seeded, chop them and transfer them to a bowl along with any captured juices.

In a large saucepan, warm the olive oil over medium heat. Add the onion, garlic, star anise, cinnamon, and coriander and sweat the onion until tender, about 5 minutes. Add the tomatoes and their juice, raise the heat to medium-high, and bring to a boil. Turn the heat to medium-low and simmer gently until thickened to a sauce consistency, 30 to 40 minutes. Add the vinegar and continue to cook, stirring every now and again to make sure the mixture is not sticking to the bottom of the pan, for about 1 hour longer. The fondue is ready when it is a little thicker than tomato sauce. Keep warm until serving.

While the fondue is cooking, make the gnocchi. Preheat the oven to 350°F. Arrange the potatoes in a single layer on a sheet pan, prick each potato a couple of times with fork tines, and bake until a skewer slid into the center of a potato meets no resistance, about 45 minutes. Remove the potatoes from the oven and let them cool until they can be handled but are still warm.

(continued next page)

Peel the potatoes and pass them through a potato ricer held over a large bowl. (You can also put the potatoes through the ricer unpeeled, but you will need to scrape the peels out of the hopper after each pass.) Let the potatoes cool until almost room temperature, then season with the salt, add the eggs, and mix thoroughly. Add half of the flour and fold it in with your hands until the flour is evenly moistened, being careful not to knead the mixture too much. Add the remaining flour and again fold in just until fully combined. Gather the dough into a rough mass.

Lightly flour a work surface and one or two sheet pans. Transfer the dough to the floured surface and knead the dough gently until smooth and soft, about 1 minute. You must not handle the dough too much or the gnocchi will be tough. Keep any dough you are not immediately working with covered with a kitchen towel to prevent it from drying out. Grasp a piece of the dough about the size of a small orange and, using your palms, roll it into a rope about 1 inch in diameter. Using a knife, cut the rope crosswise into 1-inch pieces. Pinch the center of each piece slightly, then transfer the pieces to the prepared sheet pan. Repeat until all of the dough has been rolled and cut.

Bring a large saucepan filled with salted water to a boil over high heat. Place about a dozen pieces of the cut dough into the boiling water, stir, and then wait until the gnocchi rise to the surface, which should take about 3 minutes. While the gnocchi are cooking, melt the butter in a large sauté pan over medium heat. When the gnocchi are ready, using a slotted spoon, transfer them to the sauté pan and turn them gently in the warm butter. Repeat until all of the gnocchi are cooked.

To serve, transfer the gnocchi to a warmed serving dish and spoon the warm tomato fondue over the top. Sprinkle with the Parmesan and serve immediately.

 **WINE:** *SIMI Alexander Valley Cabernet Sauvignon*

Moussaka

Moussaka, a spice-infused Mediterranean-inspired dish, has never been thought to pair well with Chardonnay or Cabernet Sauvignon. We are delighted by how it complements rosé, with its exuberant fruit and delicate hints of sweet, citrus flavors. It stands up nicely to the spicy sweetness of this classic dish of eggplant and lamb. With its vibrancy and focus, our dry rosé also offers a refreshing contrast to the umami-rich cheese and béchamel sauce that top this baked casserole.

3 globe eggplants (1 to 1¼ pounds each)
Kosher salt and freshly ground black pepper
Olive oil, for sautéing
2 large yellow onions, chopped
1 clove garlic, minced
2 pounds ground lamb
¼ teaspoon ground cinnamon
¼ teaspoon freshly grated nutmeg
2 tablespoons minced fresh flat-leaf parsley
1 tablespoon minced fresh chives
¼ teaspoon chopped fresh tarragon
1 cup homemade or canned tomato sauce
½ cup SIMI Sonoma County Dry Rosé

BÉCHAMEL
4 cups whole milk
5 tablespoons unsalted butter
¼ cup all-purpose flour
3 egg yolks (optional)
2 teaspoons kosher salt
½ teaspoon freshly grated nutmeg

2 cups grated aged Asiago cheese

Trim and peel the eggplants, then cut crosswise into ½-inch-thick slices. Sprinkle the eggplant slices on both sides with salt and place them in a single layer on paper towels to absorb the moisture. Let the eggplant slices sit while you cook the lamb mixture.

In a large sauté pan, heat about 1 tablespoon olive oil over medium heat. Add the onions and garlic and cook, stirring, until soft, 3 to 5 minutes. Add the lamb, raise the heat slightly, and cook, stirring and breaking up the meat with a wooden spoon, until browned, about 5 minutes. Add the cinnamon, nutmeg, parsley, chives, tarragon, tomato sauce, and wine and stir well. Adjust the heat to maintain a steady simmer and cook, stirring occasionally, until most of the moisture has evaporated and the flavors are well blended, about 20 minutes. Season with salt and pepper and remove from the heat.

Wipe the eggplant slices dry with paper towels. Brush a large frying pan with olive oil and place over high heat. Working in batches, fry the eggplant slices, turning them and adding more oil to the pan as needed, until browned on both sides and just tender, 2 to 3 minutes on each side. Transfer to paper towels to drain.

Preheat the oven to 350°F. Oil a 9-by-13-by-2-inch baking dish or similar-size gratin dish.

To make the béchamel, pour the milk into a saucepan and heat over medium heat just until small bubbles appear around the edge of the pan. While the milk is heating, in a heavy saucepan, melt the butter over medium heat. Whisk in the flour and continue to whisk until the mixture is bubbly and smooth, about 3 minutes. Do not allow it to color. Whisk the hot milk, 1 cup at a time, into the flour mixture, whisking until smooth after each addition.

(continued next page)

Turn the heat to medium-low and continue to cook, stirring constantly to prevent scorching, until nicely thickened, 2 to 3 minutes.

If using the egg yolks, in a medium bowl, whisk the yolks until blended. Slowly ladle about 1 cup of the hot béchamel into the eggs while whisking constantly until fully blended. Then slowly pour the egg mixture into the saucepan while whisking continuously to combine. Stir in the salt and nutmeg, remove from the heat, and keep warm.

Arrange half of the eggplant slices on the bottom of the prepared baking dish. Top with the meat mixture, spreading it evenly, and sprinkle with one-third of the cheese. Arrange the remaining eggplant slices on top and sprinkle with half of the remaining cheese. Pour the béchamel evenly over the surface and sprinkle with the remaining cheese.

Bake until bubbling is visible along the edges and the top is lightly browned, about 1 hour. Remove from the oven and let cool for 20 to 30 minutes, then cut into 3-inch squares to serve.

 **WINE:** *SIMI Sonoma County Dry Rosé*

ISABELLE'S ROSE GARDEN

South of SIMI Winery's old stone cellar is Isabelle's rose garden, said to have been planted by the SIMI heir just after her father Giuseppe's death in 1904. Isabelle purportedly planted a different rose bush for every sitting US president until she sold the winery in 1970. The only president without a rose bush was Herbert Hoover, who governed the country during Prohibition. Isabelle didn't care for him. For years, SIMI has made a dry rosé in honor of Isabelle and her rose garden.

Coconut Macaroons

This is a simple recipe that adds a sweet, finishing touch to a light spring supper. Macaroon coconut is preferred here for its fine shred, as are Tahitian vanilla beans for their beautiful floral aroma. Our SIMI 1876 Sparkling Wine is a celebratory way to end your meal, though we recommend having a macaroon first and giving your palate time to recalibrate before enjoying this relatively dry wine.

1 cup egg whites (from 7 or 8 eggs)
2 cups sugar
2½ cups macaroon coconut
½ teaspoon grated lemon zest
½ teaspoon grated orange zest
¼ cup crème fraîche or sour cream
½ Tahitian vanilla bean

In the bowl of a stand mixer, combine the egg whites and sugar. Select a saucepan in which the bowl will rest securely in the rim and fill the pan about one-fourth full with water. Bring the water to a bare simmer. Place the bowl over (not touching) the water and whisk together the egg whites and sugar just until the sugar has fully dissolved. Transfer the bowl to the mixer base, fit the mixer with the whisk attachment, and whip on high speed until the egg whites are cool and shiny, stiff peaks form.

In a large bowl, combine the coconut, lemon zest, orange zest, and crème fraîche and stir until well blended. Using a sharp knife, split the vanilla bean lengthwise, then use the tip of the knife to scrape the vanilla seeds into the coconut mixture. Stir to mix well. Remove the bowl from the mixer, spoon the egg whites on top of the coconut mixture, and fold in the egg whites just until evenly combined. Cover and refrigerate overnight.

The next day, preheat the oven to 300°F. Line a 13-by-18-inch sheet pan (half sheet pan) with parchment paper.

To shape each macaroon, use a 1-ounce ice-cream scoop, packing the coconut mixture into the scoop and then releasing it, flat side down, onto the prepared pan. The macaroon will be a half dome. Repeat until all of the coconut mixture is used up, spacing the cookies about 1 inch apart.

Bake until light golden brown, 15 to 18 minutes. Let cool completely on the pan on a wire rack, then carefully peel the cookies off of the parchment. Serve immediately or store in an airtight container at room temperature for up to 4 days.

 **WINE:** *SIMI 1876 Sparkling Wine*

INDEX

Savoring SIMI: Since 1876
Recipes and Stories from the Heart of Sonoma County
By Kolin Vazzoler and Celebrated Chefs of the SIMI Winery Kitchen

www.simiwinery.com

ISBN: 978-0-692-74795-7

Produced and designed by Jennifer Barry Design, Fairfax, California
Non-recipe text by Mora Cronin, Cronin Communications
Recipe photography by Dan Mills Productions
Food and prop styling by Joanna Badano
Recipe editorial production by Lynda Balslev
Additional photography by SIMI Winery, Brooke Barttelbort,
Jeremy Liebman, Gina Logan Photography, Scott Peterson,
and the Healdsburg Museum and Historical Society

Printed in China